At the
THRESHOLD

At the
THRESHOLD

JEWISH MEDITATIONS ON DEATH

edited by
Michael Swirsky

JASON ARONSON INC.
Northvale, New Jersey
London

Acknowledgments for permission to reprint previously published material appear on pages 161–165.

This book was set in 12 pt. Fairfield by Alpha Graphics of Pittsfield, New Hampshire.

Library of Congress Cataloging-in-Publication Data

At the threshold : Jewish meditations on death / edited by Michael
    Swirsky.
        p.   cm.
    Includes bibliographical references and index.
    ISBN 1-56821-299-2
    1. Death—Religious aspects—Judaism—Meditations.   2. Jewish
meditations.   I. Swirsky, Michael.
    BM724.A73   1996
    296.7'4—dc20   94-28742

Manufactured in the United States of America. Jason Aronson Inc. offers books and cassettes. For information and catalog write to Jason Aronson Inc., 230 Livingston Street, Northvale, New Jersey 07647.

For Santiago

Contents

Preface

This is not a book of consolation for the bereaved, although they may find some consolation in it. Nor is it intended as a didactic overview of what Judaism has to say on the subject of death, although some important Jewish teachings about death can be found here. Rather, the purpose of this small volume is to help people who are facing their own death.

Facing death is not something contemporary Western culture or the conditions of modern life encourage us to do. In former times, people would grow old or sick and die in the extended-family home, surrounded by their loved ones. Death was a normal, familiar part of life, acknowledged and prepared for. Now, life's final phases are typically hidden from view in retirement villages, nursing homes, and hospital intensive-care units, among machines and blinking lights. The dying themselves, if they are not denied the truth, are often denied the opportunity to discuss their fate with others, to voice their fears, concerns, and hopes. A great conspiracy of silence, the silence of denial, surrounds the reality of approaching death. And when life finally ends, this reality, too, is sometimes disguised by elaborate ruses and euphemisms.

Still, the dying usually know they are dying, and this fact, openly addressed or not, burns in the recesses of their every waking hour.

The Jewish tradition is one that looks squarely at the realities of human existence. Unpleasant truths, inherent in the nature of the world and ourselves, are not covered up or wished away but acknowledged and dealt with, contained and learned from, channeled, sanctified, and redeemed. Death is, of course, the unpleasant truth par excellence, the great, irreducible riddle and foil of our existence. Yet it is faced honestly—in the simple, dignified rituals of Jewish burial and mourning, in the prose of Jewish sacred wisdom, and in the poetry of Jewish prayer.

Much of Judaism's concern, in this as in other areas of life, is with human action, the application of divine imperatives and tested moral principles to the practical tasks of responsible living. That is not the concern of this book, however. It is not a halakhic treatise or a how-to book. Rather, it seeks to be helpful on the spiritual, or, as some prefer to say, existential, plane, on the level of anxiety, faith, hope, understanding, and resolve.

* * *

All of us must eventually come to terms with human mortality, the fact that built into the structure of our bodies is an absolute limitation of time. This fact, which first dawns upon us in childhood and looms gradually larger throughout life, may be forced upon our awareness quite suddenly under certain circumstances. We need then to grasp fully the implications of being mortal. And we need to console ourselves with the possibility of some kind of survival—if not of our conscious selves, then at least of some aspect of who or what we have been—beyond the frame of this earthly life.

Yet when the prospect of our own demise becomes more immediate and concrete, we may also respond with incomprehension or anger. This is, of course, particularly the case when death threatens prematurely; but how many of us, even in old age, are ever fully ready to depart this world? We protest, we argue, we rail, we negotiate. We grasp about desperately for ways to avoid or annul or deny the decree. Realizing that the decree is inescapable, we reach out for comfort. We seek consolation in our loneliness and dread, relief for our pain. Then again, the pain of terminal illness may be so great that death comes to seem a welcome release.

Finally, if we are lucky, we arrive at a point of reconciliation with our fate, a mature acceptance, this time on the deepest, most personal level, of the necessity of dying and a readiness to face its eventuality, eyes open and spirit calm. This acceptance opens the way to realistic preparation for death: taking stock of one's life, tying up loose ends, relating to the needs of those who will be left behind, deciding how to make the best possible use of the time remaining, saying goodbye.

I have tried to find words in Jewish tradition and Jewish literature—from the Bible, the Talmud, and the Midrash to the mystics, philosophers, and poets of later times—that give voice to these feelings and address these tasks. The subjective process of approaching one's demise also constitutes the structure around which this book is organized.

* * *

It will not be obvious to all readers why we should turn to tradition for help. Part of the answer, surely, lies in the great wisdom of our sages, distilled over nearly four thousand years of experience, reflection, and debate. Except for certain issues raised by very recent technology, is there any aspect of human mortality with which the Jewish tradition has not grappled, on which it does not shed light? Then, too, there is the power of the language of our forebears, its ability to help us express our deepest but, by the same token, most ineffable thoughts and emotions. Has any plea for salvation ever equalled the Psalmist's? Has any cry of impotent rage ever approached Job's? Above all, however, what tradition offers us is the possibility of transcendence: of seeing our individual plight as part of a larger framework of meaning, of finding solace for our individual woes in the fact that they are shared, recognized, uplifted.

Jewish beliefs about death, and life after death, have changed greatly over the ages. Notions such as the resurrection of the body, the survival of the soul, heaven and hell, the future world, reincarnation, and the theurgic power of prayer have made their appearance on the stage of Jewish consciousness and even remained there over long stretches of time, only to disappear or become, as most of them have for most Jews today, conventional pieties, taken with a sigh and a shrug. That is one of the reasons this book does not attempt to encompass everything Judaism has to say about death. Our focus, rather, is on those ideas and texts that seem most likely to be helpful to the contemporary reader in his or her time of need.

* * *

This is a book for the dying. Now it may be argued, who among us is *not* dying? Whether death seems but a distant prospect or is already knocking at the door, all of us must confront it eventually. Nevertheless, the impetus for compiling this reader came from real-life encounters with two people for whom the prospect of death was immediate and devastating. Both Suzy Frel and Carl Bennett were relatively young, and both suffered illnesses from which there was little chance of recovery. Both wrestled mightily not only with their illnesses but also with the spiritual problem of their own mortality. It was out of an effort to help them grapple with this problem that I came to the idea of putting together the present reader. Though for these two people the reader in its present form unfortunately comes too late, I hope that it will be helpful to others in their situation and others in my situation as their friend.

This book, I have said, owes its existence to the inspiration afforded by two people close to death. I am grateful to them for sharing with me some of their inmost feelings and thoughts and the special wisdom they were each able to wrest from their bleak predicament. I would also like to acknowledge the assistance of a number of other people in conceptualizing this book and assembling its contents. Rabbi Simon Hirschhorn helped me think the project through. Dr. Aryeh Strikowsky of the Pardes Institute, Dr. Avriel Bar-Levav of Ben-Gurion University, and Professor Ze'ev Falk of the Hebrew University guided me through the relevant Jewish literature. Rabbis Chaim Pearl, Pesach Krauss, Pesach Schindler, and Moshe Silberschein shared with me the fruits of their rich pastoral experience working with the sick and elderly. Chana Kurtzman, former dean of the Hadassah-Hebrew University School of Nursing and now of the Hadassah Mt. Scopus Hospice, gave me helpful advice. The counsel of my friend Aaron Singer, who had labored to compile a reader such as this for one much-loved individual, was especially meaningful. My thanks to Barbara Spectre, Dr. David Roskies, Dr. Simcha Paull Raphael, Dr. Avivah Zornberg, and Dr. Hava Weissler for their suggestions. And my appreciation to Dan Sharon of the Asher Library, Spertus Institute, Chicago, and the staff of the Hebrew Union College Library, Jerusalem, for their gracious assistance. I am indebted, too, to my father, Abel Swirsky, for his encouragement and criticism.

I would be grateful to readers, in turn, for their comments and suggestions, so that if subsequent editions of this book prove possible it can be made more useful to others.

Michael Swirsky

Jerusalem
Rosh Hodesh Nissan, 5754

Recognition

A Time for Everything

A season is set for everything, a time for every
    experience under heaven:
A time for being born and a time for dying,
A time for planting and a time for uprooting
    the planted;
A time for slaying and a time for healing,
A time for tearing down and a time for
    building up;
A time for weeping and a time for laughing,
A time for wailing and a time for dancing;
A time for throwing stones and a time for
    gathering stones,
A time for embracing and a time for shunning
    embraces;
A time for seeking and a time for losing,
A time for keeping and a time for discarding;
A time for ripping and a time for sewing,
A time for silence and a time for speaking;
A time for loving and a time for hating;
A time for war and a time for peace.

ECCLESIASTES

3

Over like a Sigh

O Lord, You have been our refuge
From one generation to the next.
Before the mountains were born
Or the earth or the world brought forth,
You are God, without beginning or end.

You turn men back into dust
And say: "Go back, sons of men."
To Your eyes a thousand years
Are like yesterday, come and gone,
No more than a watch in the night.

You sweep men away like a dream,
Like grass which springs up in the morning.
In the morning it springs up and flowers:
By evening it withers and fades.

So we are destroyed in Your anger,
Struck with terror at Your fury.
Our guilt lies open before You;
Our secrets in the light of Your face.

All our days pass away in Your anger.
Our life is over like a sigh.
Our span is seventy years
Or eighty for those who are strong.

And most of these are emptiness and pain.
They pass swiftly, and we are gone.
Who understands the power of Your anger
And fears the strength of Your fury?

Make us know the shortness of our life,
That we may gain wisdom of heart.

PSALMS

The Spoiler

Man enters the world and knows not why,
He rejoices but knows not the reason,
He lives and knows not how long.
In childhood he behaves stubbornly,
And when in its time desire arises,
Arousing him to the pursuit of power and wealth,
He sets out from his place,
Sailing the seas and traversing the deserts,
Venturing into lions' dens
And exposing himself to wild beasts.
And when he imagines his glory to be great,
His attainments mighty,
Quietly the spoiler steals up on him.
He opens his eyes, and all is gone.
He is forever prone to troubles
That pass and return,
Every day, mishaps,
Every hour, setbacks,
Every moment, terrors.
Should he rest content,
Disaster will suddenly overtake him.
Either war will come and a sword smite him,
Or he will be run through by a bronze spear,

Or he will be encompassed by sorrows,
Swallowed up by raging waters,
Or he will be visited by awful, lingering diseases,
Till he becomes a burden to himself,
His honey laced with venom.
As his pain grows, his glory diminishes.
The young mock him, mere children order him
    about.
He becomes a burden to his offspring,
And his friends are estranged from him.
When his hour comes, he leaves
His own courts for the court of perdition,
The shade of his rooms for the shadow of death.
He takes off his fancy crimson garments
And puts on rot and decay.
He lies down in the dust,
Returning to the base from which he was hewn.
The person whom all this befalls—
When shall he find time to repent,
To scrub off the rust of his misdeeds?
For the day is short and the work much,
And the taskmasters rush angrily about.
Time laughs at him,
And the Master of the House is impatient.
So I beg You, O God, to remember
The distress we humans must endure,
And if I have done wrong,
Make good my end.

Do not repay measure for measure
One whose sins are without measure,
Who, dying, departs without joy.

SOLOMON IBN GABIROL

At the Abyss

At the edge of the abyss of your existence you
    stand.
Knowing how far from wise you are,
How far from possible any human wisdom is.
Knowing you are a driven leaf, a passing shadow in
    this world.
Standing there, you exist, you dream.
You say a word, perhaps hear a word,
And silence once again prevails.
And you try again, return again to the beginning,
And in the end, the beginning is the end.

Pinhas Sadeh

Life and Death Are Brothers

O my soul, set your heart toward the highway, the way by which you have walked; for all was made of dust, and indeed all shall return to dust. Everything that was created and fashioned has an end and a goal, to return to the ground from which it was taken. Life and death are brothers that dwell together; they cling together and cannot be drawn apart. They are joined together by the two ends of a frail bridge over which all created beings pass: life is the way in, and death is the way out; life builds, and death demolishes; life sows, and death reaps; life plants, and death uproots; life unites, and death separates; life links together, and death scatters.

Therefore know and see that the cup will pass over to you as well, and you shall soon go from the lodging place that is on the way, when time and chance befall you and you return to your eternal home. On that day you shall delight in your work and take your reward for the labor in which you toiled, whether it be good or bad. . . .

O my soul, prepare provisions in abundance. Prepare not little while you are yet alive and your hand has strength, because the journey is too great for you.

And do not say, "Tomorrow will I make provision," for the day has declined and you know not what the next day may bring. Know also that yesterday will never return and that whatever you have done then is weighed, numbered, and counted. And do not say, "Tomorrow I will do it," for the day of death is hidden from all the living. . . .

Seek the Lord your Maker with all your might and strength. Seek righteousness, seek meekness. . . . Now arise, go and pray to the Lord, and take up a song to your God. . . .

BAHYA IBN PAKUDA

A Narrow Bridge

Know that a person has to pass through this world as if he were crossing the narrowest of bridges. But the bridge is wide enough to carry one across. The main thing is not to be afraid.

RABBI NAHMAN OF BRATSLAV

Living toward Death

The river of life, even when it flows without impediment, flows always away from the sources that gave rise to it, on and on until it reaches the sea. It doesn't return on itself. Life is not eternal. It flows from birth toward death. . . . Life lives itself toward death. . . .

Each step is attended by fear. It should not be so. Courage in facing life should silence the fear. Nor is this fear any longer a fear of life. . . . It is rather anxiety about the step that has been taken. About the lived life, which, now that it has been lived, belongs to death. Anxiety turns into disappointment. . . . Disappointment turns into weariness. . . .

It is so difficult to know that all verification lies ahead, to know that only death will verify. That it is the ultimate proving ground of life. And that being able to live means being compelled to die.

He who withdraws himself from life may think that he has withdrawn himself from death, but he has actually withdrawn only from life, and death, which he meant to elude, now surrounds him on all sides. It has crept into his heart, which has been turned to stone. If he is to be restored to life he must acknowledge the dominion of death. He must no longer wish to live otherwise than deathward. Life becomes simple then, indeed, but only because it does not seek to elude death. . . .

There is no cure for death. Not even health. But the healthy man has the strength to walk alive to his grave. The sick man invokes Death, and lets himself be carried on his back, half-dead from fear of him. Health experiences even Death only "at the right time." It is good friends with him, and it knows that when he comes he will remove the rigid mask and take the flickering torch from the hands of his frightened, weary, disappointed brother, Life. He'll dash it to the ground and extinguish it, and only then, under the skies that flame up for the first time when the torch has been extinguished, he'll enfold the swooning one in his arms, and only then, when Life has closed its eloquent lips, he'll open his eternally silent mouth and say: "Do you recognize me? I am your brother."

FRANZ ROSENZWEIG

Beyond Time

If we look truthfully at the loss of time and see how quickly it slips through our fingers, leaving us not a moment's rest or peace, we will see that time really does not exist. It is but an illusion, resulting from the limited nature of our minds. Similarly, in a dream, one can imagine that seventy years have passed but then, upon awakening, realize that it was only a quarter of an hour. . . . Recognizing the unreality of time, one understands that it is futile to be caught up in timebound hopes; one should rather aspire to that which is beyond time. And believing in this category, "beyond time," one will never fall; for all falling is a function of time.

RABBI NAHMAN OF BRATSLAV

Surviving as a Thought of God

Awareness of God is awareness of being thought of by God, of being an object of His concern, of His expectation.

Surviving after death, we hope, is surviving as a thought of God.

The question that looms in relation to my own self is: Am I worthy of surviving, of being a thought of God? What is it about myself or my existence that has affinity to eternity?

Survival beyond death carries, according to Judaism, demands and obligations during life here and now. Conditions are attached to the hope of survival.

Eternity is not an automatic consequence of sheer being, and survival is not an unconditional epilogue of living. It must be achieved, earned. . . .

Marvelous and beautiful is life in the body, but more marvelous and more beautiful is life in a word. The word is greater than the world; by the word of God all was created. The Book, Scripture, is an everlasting constellation of holy words. When a good man dies, his soul becomes a word and lives in God's book. . . .

We must distinguish between being human and human being. We are born human beings. What we must acquire is being human. Being human is the essential, the decisive achievement of a human being.

Human being finds its end in organic dissolution. But being human is not an organic substance; it is an action and a radiance of the personhood of man. The unity, the sum total of moments of personhood, is a presence that goes on in terms surpassing mere existence. . . .

The meaning of existence is in the sanctification of time, in lending eternity to the moments. Being human is a quest for the lasting. . . .

It is a distortion to characterize the life of man as moving toward death. Death is the end of the road, and while moving along the long road of days and nights, we are really moving toward living, acting, achieving. Death is the end of the road, but not its meaning, not a refutation of living. That every moment of life is a step toward death is a mechanical view. . . . Those who say that we die every day, that every moment deprives us of a portion of life, look at moments as time past. Looking at moments as time present, every moment is a new arrival, a new beginning. . . .

Death is the end of what we can do in being partners to redemption. The life that follows must be earned while we are here. It does not come out of nothing; it is an ingathering, the harvest of eternal moments achieved while on earth. . . .

The greatest problem is not how to continue but how to exalt our existence. The cry for a life beyond the grave is presumptuous if there is no cry for eternal life prior to our descending to the grave. Eternity is not perpetual future but perpetual presence. He has planted in us the seed of eternal life. The world to come is not only a hereafter but also a herenow.

ABRAHAM JOSHUA HESCHEL

The Living

"The Lord said to Moses, 'Your days are drawing near to die'" (Deuteronomy 31:14).

Said Shmuel bar Nahmani: Do days die? What it means is that, at the death of the righteous, their days cease from the world, but they themselves remain, as it says, "In whose hand is the soul of all the living" (Job 12:10).

Can this mean that the living alone are in God's hand and not the dead? No, it means that the righteous, even after their death, may be called living, while the wicked, both in life and in death, may be called dead.

TANHUMA

19

With Our Lives We Give Life

Eternal God, the generations come and go before You. Brief is their time. Passing, they leave many of their tasks unfinished, their plans unfulfilled, their dreams unrealized. It would be more than we could bear, but for the faith that our little day finds its permanence in Your eternity and our work its completion in the unfolding of Your purpose for humanity.

As night follows day, the candle of our life burns down and gutters. There is an end to the flames. Yet we do not despair, for we are more than a memory slowly fading into the darkness. With our lives we give life.

Early or late, all must answer the summons to return to the Reservoir of Being. For we loosen our hold on life when our time has come, as the leaf falls from the bough when its day is done. The deeds of the righteous enrich the world, as the fallen leaf enriches the soil beneath.

GATES OF PRAYER

Parents and Children

Rabbi Pinhas bar Hama expounded: In the verse "When Hadad heard in Egypt that David slept with his fathers, and that Joab the captain of the host was dead" (1 Kings 11:21), why is the term "slept" used in the case of David and "dead" in the case of Joab? It is said that David "slept" because he had a son; it is said that Joab "was dead" because he left no son.

Did Joab not leave a son? Surely it is written, "Of the sons of Joab . . ." (Ezra 8:9)!

David, who left a son like himself, is said to have "slept"; Joab, who did not leave a son like himself, "was dead."

BABA BATRA

The People's Soul

"He is gathered to his people" (Genesis 25:8). . . .
"And you shall go to your fathers" (Genesis 15:15).
. . . If man enters into the abode of his fathers, he is
thereby elevated above the character of an individual
being. . . .

It is the *people*, it is the people's soul into which
the individual soul enters. The people does not die
but has a history which continues. And *history*, the
history of one's people, gives duration and continu-
ity to the individual soul.

Immortality acquires the meaning of the historical living-on of the individual in the historical conti-
nuity of his people.

HERMANN COHEN

The Chain of the Generations

One day, Honi the Circle-Drawer was going along the road when he saw a man planting a carob tree. "How long," he asked him, "will it take for this tree to bear fruit?"

"Seventy years," the man replied.

"Are you sure you will live another seventy years?"

He answered, "When I came into this world I found carob trees already full-grown. Just as my forebears planted them for me, so do I plant this for my children."

TA'ANIT

Repaying God

We have been given so much. Why is the outcome of our lives, the sum of our achievements, so little?

Our embarrassment is like an abyss. Whatever we give away is so much less than what we receive. Perhaps this is the meaning of dying: to give one's whole life away.

Our greatest problem is not how to continue but how to return. "How can I repay unto the Lord all His bountiful dealings with me?" (Psalm 116:12). When life is an answer, death is a homecoming. "Precious in the sight of the Lord is the death of His saints" (Psalm 116:14). . . .

This is the meaning of death: the ultimate self-dedication to the divine. Death so understood will not be distorted by the craving for immortality, for this act of giving away is reciprocity on man's part for God's gift of life. For the pious man, it is a privilege to die.

ABRAHAM JOSHUA HESCHEL

Protest

Against Your Will

Before the formation of the embryo in its mother's womb, the Holy One decrees what it is to be in the end—male or female, weak or strong, poor or rich, short or tall, ungainly or handsome, scrawny or fat, humble or insolent. He also decrees what is to happen to it, but not whether it is to be righteous or wicked, a matter He places solely in the man's power.

He beckons the angel in charge of spirits and says to him, "Bring Me such-and-such a spirit, which is in the Garden of Eden, is called So-and-so, and whose appearance is thus-and-so." At once, the angel goes and brings the spirit to the Holy One. When the spirit arrives, it bows and prostrates itself before the King who is King of Kings, the Holy One, blessed be He.

In that instant the Holy One says to the spirit, "Enter the drop that is in such-and-such angel's hand." The spirit opens its mouth and says, "Master of the universe, the world in which I have been dwelling since the day You created me is enough for me. Why do You wish to have me, who am holy and pure, hewn from the mass of Your glory, enter this fetid drop?" The Holy One replies, "The world I will have you enter will be more beautiful for you than the one in which you have dwelled. Indeed, when I formed you, I formed you only for this drop." With that the Holy One makes the spirit enter the drop against its will. Then the angel returns and has the [drop of semen with the] spirit enter the mother's womb. Moreover, two angels are designated for the spirit to guard it, so that it will not leave the embryo or fall out of it. There a lamp is lit over its head, and it is able to look and see from one end of the world to the other. . . .

Then the angel strolls with the spirit from morning till evening and shows it the place where it is to die and the place where it is to be buried. The angel continues strolling with it throughout the world, showing it the righteous and the wicked, and finally shows it everything. In the evening the angel returns the spirit to its mother's womb, and there the Holy One provides bolted gates for it. The embryo lies in its mother's womb for nine months. . . .

In the end, its time comes to go forth into the world. The same angel appears and says to the spirit, "Your time to go forth into the air of the world has come." The spirit: "Why do you wish to take me out into the air of the world?" The angel: "My child, know that you will be born against your will, will die against your will, and against your will are to give an account and reckoning before the King who is King of Kings, the Holy One, blessed be He."

But the spirit refuses to go out of the womb, so that the angel has to beat it and put out the lamp that has been burning over its head, and then he brings it forth into the world against its will. Instantly, the infant forgets all that he has seen . . . and all that he has known. Why does the infant weep as he goes forth? Because he has lost a place of repose and comfort; [he weeps] for the world which he was compelled to leave.

When a man's time to die comes, the same angel appears to him and asks, "Do you recognize me?" The man answers, "Yes," and proceeds to inquire, "Why did you come this day and not on any other day?" The angel: "To take you out of the world. Your time to depart has arrived." The man begins to weep and makes his voice heard from one end of the world to the other. But his fellow creatures are not aware of it, because they cannot hear his voice. . . . The man pleads with the angel, "You have already taken me out of two worlds and made me enter this world." The angel: "Have I not told you that you were formed against your will, were born against your will, were alive against your will, and against your will are destined to give an account and reckoning before the Holy One, blessed be He?"

TANHUMA

Departing

The world, which was made for us, abides, but we, for whom it was made, depart.

2 Barukh

Rabbi El'azar said: Even if a man were to live a thousand years, at the time of his departure from the world it would seem to him as if he had only lived a single day.

Zohar

Pleading for Time

"And the Lord said to Moses, 'The time is drawing near for you to die'" (Deuteronomy 31:14). These words are to be considered in the light of the verse "Though his excellency mount up to the heavens, and his head reach unto the clouds, yet he shall perish. . . . They that have seen him shall say, 'Where is he?'" (Job 20:6–7). To whom does this verse refer? To none other than [to him who nears] the day of death. Even if a man should make himself wings like a bird and go up to heaven, once his time comes to die, his wings will be broken and he will fall down.

When Moses realized that the decree [of death] had been sealed against him, he drew a small circle around himself, stood in it, and said, "Master of the Universe, I will not budge from here until You void that decree." At the same time, he donned sackcloth—indeed, wrapped himself in it—strewed ashes upon himself, and persisted in prayer and supplication before the Holy One. . . .

What did the Holy One do then? He had it proclaimed at every gate of every firmament that Moses' prayer be not accepted nor brought up to His presence, because the decree concerning him had been sealed. Still, as the sound of Moses' prayer to Him above grew even stronger, the Holy One summoned the ministering angels and commanded them, "Go down in haste, and bolt all the gates of every firmament"—for Moses' prayer was like a sword, ripping and tearing, and nothing could stop it.

In that instant, Moses said to the Holy One, "Master of the Universe, known and revealed to You is the trouble and pain I suffered on account of Israel, until they came to believe in Your Name. How much pain I suffered because of them, until I inculcated among them the Torah and its precepts! I said to myself: As I witnessed their woe, so will I be allowed to witness their weal. Yet now that Israel's weal has come, You tell me, 'You shall not go over this Jordan' (Deuteronomy 3:27). Thus Your Torah, which asserts, 'You must pay him his wages on the same day' (Deuteronomy 24:15), You manifestly turn into a fraud. Is such the reward for the forty years of labor that I labored until Israel became a holy people, loyal to their faith?" The Holy One, replied, "Nevertheless, such is the decree that has gone forth from My Presence!" . . .

Then Moses went to the Angel of the Presence and implored, "Entreat mercy on my behalf, that I not die." The angel replied, "Moses, my master, of what avail is this effort? For I have heard from behind the curtain above that your prayer in this matter will not be heard." Moses put his hands on his head and lamented and wept, as he said, "To whom am I to go now to entreat mercy in my behalf?" In that instant the Holy One was filled with anger at Moses. . . .

Nevertheless, Moses said to God: "Master of the Universe, shall the feet that went up to the firmament, the face that confronted the Presence, the hands that received the Torah from Your hand—shall these now lick dust?" The Holy One replied: "Such was My thought [from the very beginning], and such must be the way of the world: each generation is to have its own interpreters of Scripture, each generation is to have its own providers, each generation is to have its own leaders. . . ."

Moses pleaded with the Holy One, "Master of the Universe, for my sake, remember the day when You revealed Yourself to me at the bush; for my sake, remember the time when I stood on Mount Sinai forty days and forty nights. I beg You, do not hand me over to the Angel of Death." Again a divine voice came forth and said, "Fear not, I Myself will attend you and your burial."

Moses pleaded, "Then wait until I bless Israel. On account of the warnings and reprimands I heaped upon them, they never found any ease with me." Then he began to bless each tribe separately, but when he saw that time was running short, he included all the tribes in a single blessing.

Then he said to Israel, "Because of the Torah and

its precepts, I troubled you greatly. Now please forgive me." They replied, "Our master, our lord, you are forgiven." In their turn they said to him, "Moses our teacher, we troubled you even more; we made your burden so heavy. Please forgive us." Moses replied, "You are forgiven."

Again a divine voice came forth: "The moment has come for you to depart from this world." Moses replied, "Blessed be His Name! May He live and endure forever and ever!" Then he said to Israel, "I implore you, when you enter the Land, remember me and my bones, and say, 'Alas for the son of Amram, who had run before us like a horse, yet his bones fell in the wilderness.'"

Again a divine voice came forth and said, "Within half a moment you are to depart from the world." Moses lifted both his arms, placed them over his heart, and called out to Israel, "Behold the end of flesh and blood." Moses arose and washed his hands and feet and thus became as pure as a seraph.

Then, from the highest heaven of heavens, the Holy One came down to take the soul of Moses, and with Him the three ministering angels, Michael, Gabriel, and Zagzagel. Michael laid out his bier, and Gabriel spread a fine linen cloth at his head, while Zagzagel spread it at his feet. Michael stood at one side and Gabriel at the other. Then the Holy One said to Moses, "Moses, close your eyes," and he closed his eyes. "Put your arms over your breast," and he put his arms over his breast. "Bring your legs together," and he brought his legs together.

Then the Holy One summoned Moses' soul saying, "My daughter, I had fixed the time for your sojourn in the body of Moses at a hundred and twenty years. Now your time has come to depart. Depart. Delay not." She replied, "Master of the Universe, I know that You are God of all spirits and Lord of all souls. You created me and placed me in the body of Moses one hundred and twenty years ago. Is there a body in the world more pure than the body of Moses? I love him, and I do not wish to depart from him." The Holy One exclaimed, "Depart, and I will take you up to the highest heaven of heavens and will set you under the Throne of Glory, next to the cherubim and seraphim."

In that instant, the Holy One kissed Moses and took his soul with that kiss.

At that, the holy spirit wept and said, "Never again did there arise in Israel a prophet like Moses" (Deuteronomy 34:10).

The heavens wept and said, "The godly man is perished from the earth" (Micah 7:2).

The earth wept and said, "The upright among men is no more" (Micah 7:2).

The ministering angels wept and said, "He executed the righteousness of the Lord" (Deuteronomy 33:21).

Israel wept and said, "His decisions are for Israel" (Deuteronomy 33:21).

These as well as those said together, "Let him come to peace and have rest on his couch" (Isaiah 57:2).

DEUTERONOMY RABBAH, TANHUMA, YALKUT SHIM'ONI

What Is the Measure
of My Days?

I was dumb, silent;
   I was very still
   while my pain was intense.
My mind was in a rage,
   my thoughts were all aflame;
   I spoke out:
   Tell me, O Lord, what my term is,
   what is the measure of my days;
   I would know how fleeting my life is.
You have made my life just handbreadths long;
   its span is as nothing in Your sight;
   no man endures any longer than a breath.
Man walks about as a mere shadow;
   mere futility is his hustle and bustle,
   amassing and not knowing who will gather in.
What, then, can I count on, O Lord?
In You my hope lies.

PSALMS

The Angel of Death at Bay

"Tell me, O Lord, what my term is, what is the measure of my days" [Psalm 39:5]. When David pleaded with the Holy One, "Master of the Universe, let me know when my term is to be up," God replied, "This decree has gone forth from Me: the end of a mortal is not to be made known to him."

"What is the measure of my days?"

"This decree has gone forth from Me: a man's span of life is not to be made known to him."

"Let me know the day I will cease to be."

God replied, "You will die on the Sabbath."

"Let me die on the first day of the week."

"By then the time for the reign of Solomon your son will have come, and one reign may not overlap another even by a hairsbreadth."

"Then let me die on the sixth day of the week."

God replied, "[Remember your saying,] 'Better one day in Your courts than a thousand [anywhere else]' [Psalm 84:11]? So too, for Me, the one extra [Sabbath] day you sit in the courts [of study] where you occupy yourself with Torah is better than the thousand burnt offerings your son Solomon will bring to Me on the altar."

Hence, every Sabbath David would sit and study Torah all day. On the day that his time to die came, the Angel of Death stationed himself before David, but he could not prevail, because learning did not cease from his mouth. The Angel of Death said to himself, "What am I to do with him?"

Now behind David's house there was a garden. So the Angel of Death entered it, then flew up and made a moaning sound in the trees. David went out to see [what caused the sound]. As he climbed the ladder, it broke under him [and, silenced for an instant, learning ceased]. At that, his soul left him, and he died.

SHABBAT, ECCLESIASTES RABBAH

The Fears of the Righteous

When the followers of the Rabbi of Kobryn sat around his table on the festival of Shavuot, he said to them: "It is written that at Mount Sinai the people said to Moses, 'You speak with us and we will hear; but let not God speak with us, lest we die.' How is it possible that in their greatest hour Israel refused to hear the voice of God for fear of death, which is nothing but a wresting of the soul from its husk to cling to the light of life?"

Over and over again, and more and more earnestly, the *tzaddik* repeated his question. The third time he uttered it, he fainted away and lay motionless a while. It took them a long time to revive him, but then he straightened up in his chair and concluded his teaching: "'. . . Lest we die'—for it was very hard for them to give up serving God on earth."

HASIDIC LORE

Alive He Shall
Acknowledge You

Alive alive he shall acknowledge You
Sings my soul
The wild bird that refuses
To become a statue
Impervious to frost
Its thoughts a bronze coating
A permanent coating.

The madness of life shall acknowledge You
Cast at the day of death,
Sings the blood of my heart
That refuses to turn to dew
And dissolve in beauty,
Sings the hot blood of my heart.

· ZELDA

From the Grave,
Who Can Give You Praise?

Have mercy on me, Lord; I have no strength;
Lord, heal me, my body is racked;
My soul is racked with pain.

But You, O Lord . . . how long?
Return, Lord, rescue my soul!
Save me in Your merciful love.
For in death no one remembers You;
From the grave, who can give You praise?

I am exhausted with my groaning;
Every night I drench my pillow with tears;
I bedew my bed with weeping.
My eye wastes away with grief.

PSALMS

What Is to Be Gained
from My Death?

When I was untroubled,
   I thought, "I shall never be shaken,"
   for You, O Lord, when You were pleased,
   made me firm as a mighty mountain.
When You hid Your face,
   I was terrified.
I called to You, O Lord;
   to my Lord I made appeal,
   "What is to be gained from my death,
   from my descent into the Pit?
Can dust praise You?
Can it declare Your faithfulness?
Hear, O Lord, and have mercy on me;
   O Lord, be my help!"

PSALMS

Is It for Your Sake?

Whenever Rabbi Levi Yitzhak came to that passage in the Haggadah of Passover which deals with the Four Sons and in it read about the fourth son, about "the one who knows not how to ask," he said, "'The one who knows not how to ask'—that is myself, Levi Yitzhak of Berditchev. I do not know how to ask You, Lord of the World, and even if I did know, I could not bear to do it. How could I venture to ask You why everything happens as it does, why we are driven from one exile into another, why our foes are allowed to torment us so.

"But in the Haggadah, the father of him 'who knows not how to ask' is told, 'It is for you to disclose it to him.' And the Haggadah refers to the Scriptures, in which it is written, 'And you shall tell your son.' And, Lord of the World, am I not Your son?

"I do not beg You to reveal to me the secret of Your ways—I could not bear it! But show me one thing; show it to me more clearly and more deeply; show me what this that is happening at this very moment means to me, what it demands of me, what You, Lord

44

of the World, are telling me by way of it. Ah, it is not why I suffer that I wish to know, but only whether I suffer for Your sake."

HASIDIC LORE

Consider My Sorrows
with My Sins

O my God,
If my sin is too great to bear,
What will You do for Your great name's sake?
And if I cannot hope for Your mercy,
Who else will pity me?
Therefore, though You slay me, I will trust in You.
For if You pursue my iniquity,
I will flee from You to Yourself,
Sheltering myself from Your wrath in Your own
    shadow,
And take hold of the skirts of Your mercies
Until You take pity on me.
I will not let You go till You bless me.
Remember, I pray, that You fashioned me out of
    clay
And tried me with all these hardships.
Do not, then, visit my misdeeds upon me
Or feed me the fruit of my actions,
But be patient, and bring not my day,
Until I have prepared provisions for the way back.
Do not press me to leave this world while
I still bear the kneading trough of my sins on my
    shoulder.

And when You place my sins in the balance,
Place my sorrows in the other pan.
Remembering my wickedness and rebelliousness,
Recall my suffering and misery,
And place these opposite those.
Remember, too, my God, that You sent me
    wandering
And tried me in the furnace of exile.
You have refined me from the mass of my illdoing,
I know that it is for my good that You have
    tested me
And in faithfulness made me suffer,
That it was to profit me in the end
That You took me through these tribulations.
Therefore, O God, let Your mercy be stirred
    toward me.
Do not expend Your anger upon me,
And do not reward me according to my deeds.
Tell the destroying angel, Enough!
For what height or advantage have I attained
That You should pursue me for my sins,
Posting a watch for me
And catching me like an animal in a trap?
Are not most of my days past and gone?
Shall the rest be consumed in their iniquity?
If I am here today before You,
"Tomorrow Your eyes will be upon me, and I shall
    not be."

47

"Why, now, should I die, this great fire
    consuming me?"
My God, gaze kindly upon me
For the brief remainder of my days,
And do not pursue the fugitive survivors.
Let not the crops spared by the hail
Be consumed by locusts for my sins.
For I am the creation of Your hands:
Of what use would it be to You for worms
To feed on me, the work of Your hands?

SOLOMON IBN GABIROL

God Is Against Me

I am the man who has known affliction
Under the rod of His wrath;
Me He drove on and on
In unrelieved darkness;
On none but me He brings down His hand
Again and again, without cease.
He has worn away my flesh and skin;
He has shattered my bones.
All around me He has built
Misery and hardship;
He has made me dwell in darkness,
Like those long dead.
He has walled me in and I cannot break out;
He has weighed me down with chains.
And when I cry and plead,
He shuts out my prayer;
He has walled in my ways with hewn blocks,
He has made my paths a maze.

LAMENTATIONS

Better to Die

Perish the day on which I was born,
And the night it was announced,
"A male has been conceived!"
May that day be darkness.

Why does He give light to the sufferer
And life to the bitter in spirit,
To those who wait for death but it does not come,
Who search for it more than for treasure,
Who rejoice to exultation
And are glad to reach the grave,
To the man who has lost his way,
Whom God has hedged about?

My groaning serves as my bread;
My roaring pours forth as water.
For what I feared has overtaken me;
What I dreaded has come upon me.
I had no repose, no quiet, no rest,
And trouble came.

Would that my request were granted,
That God gave me what I wished for;

Would that God consented to crush me,
Loosed His hand and cut me off.
Then this would be my consolation,
As I writhed in unsparing pains:
That I did not suppress my words against the Holy
 One.
What strength have I, that I should endure?
How long have I to live, that I should be patient?
Is my strength the strength of rock?
Is my flesh bronze?
Truly, I cannot help myself;
I have been deprived of resourcefulness.

JOB

Look Away from Me!

What is man, that You make much of him,
That You fix Your attention upon him?
You inspect him every morning,
Examine him every minute.
Will You not look away from me for a while,
Let me be, till I swallow my spittle?
If I have sinned, what have I done to You,
Watcher of men?
Why make me Your target,
And a burden to myself?
Why do You not pardon my transgression
And forgive my iniquity?
For soon I shall lie down in the dust;
When You seek me, I shall be gone.

JOB

52

I Cry to You in Vain

Terror tumbles upon me;
It sweeps away my honor like the wind;
My dignity vanishes like a cloud.
So now my life runs out;
Days of misery have taken hold of me.
By night my bones feel gnawed;
My sinews never rest.
With great effort I change clothing;
The neck of my tunic fits my waist.
He regarded me as clay.
I have become like dust and ashes.
I cry out to You but You do not answer me;
I wait, but You do not consider me.
You have become cruel to me;
With Your powerful hand You harass me.
You lift me up and mount me on the wind;
You make my courage melt.
I know You will bring me to death,
The house assigned for all the living.

JOB

53

Suffering

Heal Me and I Shall Be Healed

Heal me, O Lord, and I shall be healed,
Save me, and I shall be saved.
Bind up my wounds and ease my pain.
Shelter me in Your great peace.
Grant, I beg You, that I may yet
Keep Your commandments and uphold Your laws.
Let me be among those who find refuge
In the shadow of Your wings,
Who enjoy the choice food of Your house
And drink from the stream of Your delights.
May I merit the great beneficence
You have stored up for those who revere You,
Have wrought for those who take refuge in You.
For You are the source of life,
And in Your light shall we be illumined.
To him who asks of You but a little
You give double measure or more.
For Your servant asks according to
His weakness and crushed spirit,
But You shower good upon us
According to Your might and power.
O God, our salvation,
We shall thank You always

And praise You throughout the generations.
Blessed are You forever.
Amen and amen.

SAADYA GAON

All My Body Is Sick

O Lord, do not rebuke me in Your anger;
Do not punish me, Lord, in Your rage.
Your arrows have sunk deep in me;
Your hand has come down upon me.
Through Your anger all my body is sick;
Through my sin, there is no health in my limbs.

My guilt towers higher than my head;
It is a weight too heavy to bear.
My wounds are foul and festering,
The result of my own folly.
I am bowed and brought to my knees.
I go mourning all the day long.

All my frame burns with fever;
All my body is sick.
Spent and utterly crushed,
I cry aloud in anguish of heart.

O Lord, You know all my longing:
My groans are not hidden from You.
My heart throbs, my strength is spent;
The very light has gone from my eyes. . . .

O Lord, do not forsake me!
My God, do not stay afar off!
Make haste and come to my help,
O Lord, my God, my savior!

PSALMS

To Feel the Darkness

To feel the darkness hammer on the eyeballs;
  To thrust blind fingers into empty space;
To start in terror when the bushes rustle;
  To pray for miracles and long for grace;

Seven times to hope what seven times was
  abandoned;
  From "Never, never," to "But a little wait";
To alternate 'twixt waking and oblivion;
  To curse my fate and to accept my fate;

To seek asylum in the lap of memory,
  To cling to her dear, loving folds in vain;
To shake with pain, or lie in drunken stupor
  Until the day breaks through the window-pane.

RAHEL

Through the Openings

My soul peered through the openings
In the desolation and emptiness
Of my sickness.
It called out from its captivity
To Him who was, is, and shall be,
In the dark it whispered:
Into Your hand I entrust my spirit, my pain,
My honor, my life, my death.

ZELDA

I Am Sinking

Save me, O God,
For the waters have risen to my neck.

I have sunk into the mud of the deep
And there is no foothold.
I have entered the waters of the deep,
And the waves overwhelm me.

I am weary with all my crying;
My throat is parched.
My eyes are wasted away
From looking for my God. . . .

Rescue me from sinking in the mud;
Save me from my foes.

Save me from the waters of the deep.
Lest the waves overwhelm me.
Do not let the deep engulf me
Nor death close its mouth on me.

Lord, answer, for Your love is kind;
In Your compassion, turn towards me.

Do not hide Your face from Your servant;
Answer quickly, for I am in distress.

PSALMS

Restore Me to Health

I beg You, O Lord, healer of all flesh,
Have mercy upon me
And support me in Your grace
Upon my bed of sickness.
Send relief and healing to me
And to all who are sick.

Grant wisdom to the physician,
That he may cure my ailment
And restore me speedily to health.
Let me complete my years in wholeness,
So that I can serve You
And keep Your commandments with a perfect heart.

Help me to understand that this bitter trial
Has come upon me for my welfare,
So that I do not despise Your discipline
Or weary of Your reproof.
O God of forgiveness, gracious and merciful,
Slow to anger and abundantly kind,
I turn to You in penitence.
Help me avoid the path of folly
And walk before You henceforth in truth.

Rejoice the soul of Your servant,
For unto You, O Lord, do I lift my soul.
Heal me, and I shall be healed,
Save me, and I shall be saved.

HELP AND COMFORT

Withered like the Grass

O Lord, listen to my prayer;
And let my cry for help reach You.
Do not hide Your face from me
In the day of my distress.
Turn Your ear towards me,
And answer me quickly when I call.

For my days are vanishing like smoke,
My bones burn away like a fire.
My heart is withered like the grass.
I forget to eat my bread.
I cry with all my strength,
And my skin clings to my bones.

I have become like a pelican in the wilderness.
Like an owl in desolate places.
I lie awake and I moan
Like some lonely bird on a roof. . . .

The bread I eat is ashes;
My drink is mingled with tears.
In Your anger, Lord, and Your fury
You have lifted me up and thrown me down.

My days are like a passing shadow,
And I wither away like the grass.

Until Your Purpose
Is Fulfilled

Beloved One, watch over me today in this time of discomfort and pain. Help me to focus on healing, and soothe my soul. Bring courage and acceptance.

Blessed are You, source of life and love. Thank You for creating a world with the possibility of healing.

May it be Your will that I be healed in body and soul.

Blessed are You, sustainer of life and guide through the valley of death.

The weaker my body becomes, the stronger the fire of my soul burns. Thank You for freeing me from the distractions which prevented me from self-examination and spiritual growth.

Please, Hashem, You are the One who Heals; please heal me, too. Give direction to the doctor. Give direction to me. Let me know what I can do to get better. Give me support and strength to do whatever I need to do to heal. I will be able to do Your *mitzvot* more fully and lead a complete life.

Blessed be the Divine Presence, who holds me to Her breast when I am broken and cradles me when my body and spirit ache.

Blessed are You, creator of life, who have the power

to release me from life but sustain me for Your purpose. Give me the strength to accept this life until that purpose is fulfilled.

Although I am ill and failing, and my body is frail, thank You for still allowing me to experience the wonder and sacredness of life on this earth.

Thank You, God, for the light that is breaking through the sky, the sun that shines upon my face, my mind that is still alert despite my limitations and pain.

Through the day You will join me on this journey, so that I will never be alone or frightened, for I know You will be there. I am thankful for what I am capable of enjoying this day.

Dear God, heal my spirit, salve my pain, help to make me whole again.

Blessed is the Eternal One who gives me the ability to remember those blessings which are still mine to affirm and the strength to arise anew this day.

WHEN THE BODY HURTS, THE
SOUL STILL LONGS TO SING

Comfort Me

In both your dear hands, loving as a brother's,
    Take my own faltering hand.
You know and I know that the storm-tossed ship
    Will never make the land.

Comfort my tears with words, my only one;
    My heart is dark with pain.
You know and I know that the wandering son
    Will never see his mother's door again.

RAHEL

The Help of Others

"He feeds among the lilies" (Song of Songs 2:16).

Rabbi Yohanan suffered for three and a half years with fever. Rabbi Hanina went to visit him. He said, "How are you doing?"

He said, "It is more than I can bear."

[Rabbi Hanina] said, "Do not speak that way; say, rather, God is trustworthy."

When the pain was hard, he said, "God is trustworthy." But when the suffering became unbearable, and Rabbi Hanina went to visit him again, he spoke a [further] word to him, and he took courage.

After some while, Rabbi Hanina fell ill, and Rabbi Yohanan went to visit him. He said, "How are you doing?"

He replied, "How hard are sufferings."

Rabbi Yohanan replied, "How great is their reward."

He replied, "I desire neither them nor their reward."

Rabbi Yohanan replied, "Why do you not say to yourself the word you said to me and I took courage?"

He said, "When I was free of sufferings, I could help others; but now that I am myself a sufferer, I must ask others to help me."

Rabbi Yohanan said, "'He that feeds among the lilies': God's rod comes only upon those whose heart is soft like the lily."

SONG OF SONGS RABBAH

Be Good to Me

My strength is waning—
Be good to me, be good to me!
Be a narrow bridge for me over the abyss of
    sorrow,
Over the sorrow of my days.
Be good to me, be good to me! Be a stand-in for
    my soul,
Be a support for my heart, be a shade tree in the
    empty waste.
Be good to me! The night is so long, the dawn so
    remote.
Be a bit of light for me, be sudden joy,
Be my daily bread!

RAHEL

My Soul Is Bitter

Master of the Universe!
Open Your mouth for one dumb like me,
For one long-lost like me, for one hounded
   like me.
Help me bare my bitter heart before You.
For my soul is so very bitter
That I do not know how I can live even one more
   hour
With all the bitterness.
For I have violated the holy covenant,
The source of life.

Have pity, then, on my soul,
For it is very weary, very tired.
Splash me with cool water
To revive and restore and heal
My terribly weary soul.
It is years since the heart went out of my
   prayer,
Since I could pray with full intent
And mean the words I uttered.
It is because of this
That my soul is so very tired.

But I know that my Redeemer lives,
That He shall at last rise up triumphant.
Even now I still have hope,
Nor can there be any despair in this world.
Thus as long as my soul is in me
I shall cry out to You;
As long as there is life in me
I shall appeal for Your mercy;
As long as my spirit is in me
I shall expect and await
And hope for Your salvation.

RABBI NAHMAN OF BRATSLAV

Let Him Go

On the day Rabbi [Yehudah Hanasi] died, the rabbis proclaimed a public fast and offered prayers for divine mercy. . . .

Rabbi's maid went up to the roof and prayed, "Those above lay claim on Rabbi, and those below lay claim on him. May it be God's will that those below prevail."

But when she saw [how much he was suffering], she prayed, "May it be God's will that those above prevail."

Seeing that the rabbis were continuing to pray for divine mercy, however, she picked up a jar and threw it from the roof. They left off praying for a moment, and Rabbi's soul departed to its eternal rest.

KETUBOT

Beloved of My Soul

Beloved of my soul, merciful Father,
Draw Your servant after You to do Your will.
He would run, swift as a deer,
To kneel before Your majesty,
For Your love is sweeter to him
Than honey from the comb, than any pleasing
    savor.

Glorious, beautiful, Light of the World—
My soul is faint with love for You.
Heal her, O God, I beg You,
By letting her gaze upon Your splendor.
Then she will be healed and grow strong
And be Your slave forever.

Faithful One, let Your heart be moved with
    tenderness,
Spare the son of Your beloved friend,
For he has longed these many years
To behold Your mighty splendor.
My God, my heart's delight, oh come quickly,
Do not forsake me.

Reveal Yourself, my Dearest, and spread
Over me Your canopy of peace.
Let the earth shine with Your glory,
Let us rejoice in You.
Make haste, my Love, for the time has come;
Show me Your favor as in the days of old.

EL'AZAR AZIKRI

Acceptance

Do Not Despair!

On the Sabbath eve, [Rabbi Nahman] came from his room to the main house, where the people had assembled. He was so very, very weak that he hardly had the strength to speak. He immediately recited Kiddush over the wine and then sat down at the table. He did not return to his room after Kiddush, as was his usual custom when there were large gatherings. He sat there, in all his weakness, and feebly he began to talk a bit. He said:

". . . The main thing is this: It is forbidden to despair! . . . Even he who stands on the very bottom rung, God forbid, or in the very depths of hell, may God protect us, should nevertheless not despair. He should fulfill the Scripture: 'Out of the belly of the deep I cried' (Jonah 2:3), and be as strong as he can."

After the teaching he became very joyous and told the people to begin singing. . . . He had been so weak of late that they had hardly sung at all, but now he was so exalted that he ordered them to sing. He himself sang along with them.

Afterwards he spoke with us, very happily and with an awesome and wondrous grace. He sat through the meal with great joy, talking with us and strengthen-

ing us greatly. . . . Then he shouted from the very
depths of his heart: "*Gevalt!* Do not despair!" He went
on in these words: "There can be no despairing!"

Sihot Haran

[Rabbi Nahman] drew forth these words slowly and
deliberately, saying: "There must be no despairing."
He said the words with such strength and wondrous
depth that he taught everyone, for all generations,
that he should never despair, no matter what it is that
he has to endure.

Rabbi Nathan of Nemirov

For Good and Bad Alike

Man is bound to bless God for evil even as he blesses Him for good, for it is written, "You must love the Lord your God with all your heart and with all your soul and with all your might" (Deuteronomy 6:5). "With all your heart"—with both your good and your evil impulses. "With all your soul"—even if He takes away your soul. "With all your might"— . . . whatever treatment He metes out to you.

MISHNAH: BERAKHOT

"A man is required to bless God for evil, even as he is to bless Him for good. . . ."

What is meant by [this]? Shall I say that, just as for good one says the benediction "He who is good and bestows good," so for evil one should say the same benediction? But we have been taught: for good tidings, one says, "He who is good and bestows good"; for evil tidings, one says, "Blessed be the true Judge"!

Rava explained: What it really means is that one must accept evil with gladness. Rabbi Aha said in the name of Rabbi Levi: Where is the proof? From "I will sing of mercy and justice" (Psalm 101:1); be it "mercy," I will sing, or be it "justice," I will sing.

BERAKHOT

"Darkness is not dark for You (*mimeka*)" (Psalm 139:12)—When we know that the darkness is from You (*mimeka*), it is not darkness.

RABBI MENAHEM MENDEL OF KOTSK

Can Suffering Be Good?

Rav Huna said: "Behold, it was very good" (Genesis 1:31)—"good" refers to the measure of prosperity, "very" to the measure of suffering. But can suffering be described as "very good"? It seems incredible. But the fact is, it is through suffering that mortals come to life in the world-to-come. Indeed, Solomon said so: "Reproofs of chastisement are the way to life" (Proverbs 6:23). Go forth and see what road leads man to life in the world-to-come. You must say it is the measure of suffering.

GENESIS RABBAH

Our masters taught: When Rabbi Eliezer fell sick, four elders—Rabbi Tarfon, Rabbi Yehoshua, Rabbi El'azar ben Azariah, and Rabbi Akiva—came to visit him.

Rabbi Akiva spoke up and said, "Suffering is precious."

At that, Rabbi Eliezer said to his disciples, "Prop me up, that I may better hear the words of Akiva my disciple, who has said, 'Suffering is precious.' What proof have you, Akiva, my son, for saying it?"

Rabbi Akiva replied, "Master, I draw such inference from the verse 'Manasseh was twelve years old when he began to reign, and he reigned fifty and five years in Jerusalem . . . and he did that which was evil in the sight of the Lord' [2 Kings 21:1–2]. I consider this verse in the light of another: 'These are also the proverbs of Solomon, which the men of Hezekiah king of Judah copied out [for widespread instruction]' [Proverbs 25:1]. Now, is it conceivable that Hezekiah king of Judah taught Torah to the whole world, to all of it, but not to Manasseh, his own son? Of course not! Yet all the pains that Hezekiah took with him and all the labor that he lavished upon him did not bring him onto the right path. Only Manasseh's suffering did so, as is written, 'And the Lord spoke to Manasseh, and to his people; but they gave no heed. Wherefore the Lord brought upon them the captains and the host of the king of Assyria, who took Manasseh captive in manacles. . . . And when [Manasseh] was in distress, he besought the Lord his God and humbled himself greatly before the God of his fathers, and He answered his entreaty' [2 Chronicles 33:10–13]. You may thus infer how precious is suffering."

SANHEDRIN

Closer to God

Whoever rejoices in his suffering brings redemption to the world.

TA'ANIT

Tooth and eye are only small parts of the body, yet if they are injured the slave is given his freedom. How much more so with painful sufferings that torment a person's entire body.

BERAKHOT

One should be grateful to the Holy One, blessed be He, when suffering befalls him. Why? Because suffering draws a person toward God.

TANHUMA

The Holy One, blessed be He, brings suffering upon the righteous in this world so that they may inherit the world-to-come.

KIDDUSHIN

89

Pain Scrubs the Soul

From youth until old age, Rabbi Yitzhak Eisik suffered from an ailment which was known to involve very great pain. His physician once asked him how he managed to endure such pain without complaining or groaning. He replied, "You would understand that readily enough if you thought of the pain as scrubbing and soaking the soul in a strong solution. Since this is so, one cannot do otherwise than accept such pain with love and not grumble."

HASIDIC LORE

The word "covenant" is mentioned in connection with salt, as it is written, "You shall not omit from your meal offering the salt of your covenant with God" (Leviticus 2:13). And "covenant" is mentioned in connection with suffering, as it is written, "[The Lord will send you back to Egypt]. . . . These are the words of the covenant" (Deuteronomy 28:68–69). Just as salt cleanses meat, so does suffering wash away all a person's sins.

BERAKHOT

Into the Palace

It may be explained by way of a parable: A king had a son whom he sent to a village to be educated in the ways of the palace. When the king was informed that his son had come to maturity, out of love he sent the matron, the boy's mother, to bring him back into the palace, and there the king rejoiced with him every day.

In this way, the Holy One, blessed be He, possessed a son from the Matron, that is, the supernal holy soul. He despatched it to a village, that is, to this world, to be raised in it and initiated into the ways of the King's palace. Informed that his son had come to maturity and should be returned to the palace, the King, out of love, sent the Matron for him, to bring him.

The soul does not leave this world until such time as the Matron has arrived to get her and bring her into the King's palace, where she abides forever.

The village people wept for the departure of the king's son from among them. But one wise man said to them, "Why do you weep? Was this not the king's son, whose true place is in his father's palace, and not with you?" . . .

If the righteous were only aware of this, they would be filled with joy when their time came to leave this world. For does it not honor them greatly that the Matron comes down on their account, to take them into the King's palace, where the King may rejoice each day in them? For to God there is no joy save in the souls of the righteous.

Zohar

The Height of Knowledge

The philosophers long have taught that the forces of a young body are an impediment to most of the ethical virtues and in particular to that pure reflection which man develops from perfect knowledge, which leads to the love of God and which he cannot possibly develop out of the glowing sap of his body. The more the powers of the body subside and the fires of passion ebb, the stronger the spirit becomes, the brighter its radiance, the purer its knowledge, and the greater its joy over what it knows.

When the perfect man grows old and approaches death, this knowledge increases by leaps and bounds, and his happiness over his knowledge and his love for what he has come to know are heightened and intensified, until his soul departs from his body at the moment of greatest delight.

The sages had this in mind when, concerning the death of Moses, Aaron, and Miriam, they said that these three died through the kiss of God. . . . What [this] means is that these three died in the delights of knowledge, died of love that was all too great.

MAIMONIDES

To See God

A few days before he died, Rabbi Dov Baer, the son of Ba'al Hatanya, was joyful and happy, his holy face radiant. Over and over he was heard to utter the verse, "Into Your hands I entrust my soul."

Two hours before he died he began to preach on the subject, "With You is the source of life." Many of his leading disciples were present, and they said they had never heard him speak such pearls.

The sermon had gone on for about two hours when he came to interpreting the verse "In Your light shall we see light," and upon pronouncing these words he fell silent and discharged his soul to the care of heaven.

HASIDIC LORE

For a number of hours Rabbi Uri lay unconscious in the agony of death. His favorite disciple, Rabbi Yehudah Tzvi, opened the door from time to time, looked at the dying man, and closed the door again. At last he entered the room and went up to the bed. The next moment, the disciples who had followed him in saw their master stretch out one last time and die. Later, when they asked Rabbi Yehudah how he had known that death was imminent, he replied, "It is written, 'For man shall not see Me and live.' I saw that he saw."

HASIDIC LORE

The Next Room

Soon after the death of a *tzaddik* who was a friend of Rabbi Menahem Mendel of Vorki, one of his followers, who had been present at the death, came to him and told him about it.

"How was it?" asked Rabbi Menahem Mendel.

"Very beautiful," said the follower. "It was as though he went from one room into the next."

"From one room into the next?" said Rabbi Menahem Mendel.

"No, from one corner of the room into another corner."

HASIDIC LORE

In death, two worlds meet with a kiss: the world going out and the future coming in.

PALESTINIAN TALMUD: YEVAMOT

Into the Harbor

"A good name is better than precious oil, and the day of death better than the day of birth" (Ecclesiastes 7:1). When a person is born, all rejoice; when he dies, all weep. It should not be so. When a person is born, all should not rejoice over him, because it is not known what he will be like when grown and what his deeds will be, whether righteous or wicked, good or evil. When he dies, however, if he departs with a good name and leaves the world in peace, people should rejoice.

Rabbi Levi said: The matter may be illustrated by the parable of two vessels sailing the Mediterranean Sea, one leaving the harbor and the other entering it. As the one left the harbor, all rejoiced over it, but as the other entered the harbor, all did not rejoice. A clever man who was there said to the people, "As I see it, things should be the other way around. When a vessel leaves the harbor, all should not rejoice, because they do not know what its lot will be: what seas it will encounter, what storms it will face. But when a vessel enters the harbor all should rejoice over it, for they then know that it has come back safely from the sea and has safely entered the harbor."

It was of this that Solomon said, "The day of death is better than the day of birth."

EXODUS RABBAH

At the Proper Time

In hot weather, a rabbi delivered his discourse to his disciples under the shade of a fig tree. They noticed that each morning the owner would pick his ripened figs. "Perhaps he fears we will pick his fruit," they thought, and they moved to another place. The owner begged them to return.

Believing they had moved because his presence annoyed them, he resolved not to pick the fruit. In the evening, they saw the figs dropping from the trees, spoiled by the heat of the sun. The disciples then appreciated why it was necessary for the owner to pick them in the morning.

The rabbi said, "The owner of the figs knows when his fruit should be picked, lest it be spoiled. Thus does God know when to summon His righteous children before they are spoiled. This is the reason why many good and gracious persons are called by God at an early age."

SONG OF SONGS RABBAH

Why Should I Not Rejoice?

When Rabbi Simha Bunam of Przysucha lay dying, his wife burst into tears. He said, "What are you crying for? My whole life was only that I might learn how to die."

HASIDIC LORE

Some weeks before Rabbi Gershon Hanokh Henekh of Rodzin fell mortally ill, he spoke a great deal of death, saying that one must not be afraid of it. Even after the illness got worse, and he was in great pain, he did not groan. They asked him why this was. Perhaps by groaning he could lessen the pain, after all. He replied, "If one has complaints against the Holy One, blessed be He, he groans. If he has no complaints, he keeps quiet, accepting his suffering with love."

HASIDIC LORE

When Rabbi Elimelekh of Lizhensk perceived that his end was approaching, he possessed himself of an extraordinary cheerfulness. One of his disciples inquired the reason for his unusual mood. The rabbi thereupon took the hand of his faithful disciple into his own and said, "Why should I not rejoice, seeing that I am about to leave this world below and enter into the higher worlds of eternity? Do you not recall the words of the Psalmist, 'Though I walk through the valley of the shadow of death, I fear no harm, for You are with me' (Psalm 23:4)? Thus does the grace of God display itself."

HASIDIC LORE

Willingly

In the last two years before his death, Rabbi Yehiel Mikhal of Zloczow fell into a trance of ecstasy time after time. On these occasions, he went back and forth in his room, his face aglow with inner light, and one could see that he was clinging to a higher life rather than to earthly existence and that his soul had only to make one small step to pass into it. That is why his children were always careful to rouse him from his ecstasy at the right moment.

Once, after the third Sabbath meal, which he always had with his sons, he went to the house of study as usual and sang songs of praise. Then he returned to his room and walked up and down. At that time, no one was with him. Suddenly his daughter, who was passing his door, heard him repeat over and over, "Willingly did Moses die. Willingly did Moses die." She was greatly troubled and called one of her brothers.

When he entered, he found his father lying on the floor on his back and heard him whisper the last word of the confession, "One," with his last breath.

HASIDIC LORE

102

Take Me, O Lord

Several years before Abraham Heschel's death in 1972, he suffered a near-fatal heart attack from which he never fully recovered. I traveled to his apartment in New York to see him. He had gotten out of bed for the first time to greet me and was sitting in the living room when I arrived, looking weak and pale. He spoke slowly and with some effort, almost in a whisper. I strained to hear his words.

"Sam," he said, "when I regained consciousness, my first feelings were not of despair or anger. I felt only gratitude to God for my life, for every moment I had lived. I was ready to depart. 'Take me, O Lord,' I thought, 'I have seen so many miracles in my lifetime.'"

Exhausted by the effort, he paused for a moment, then added, "That is what I meant when I wrote [in the preface to his book of Yiddish poems], 'I did not ask for success; I asked for wonder. And You gave it to me.' . . ."

Leaving Heschel's home, I walked alone, in silence, aimlessly, oblivious of others, depressed by the knowledge that the man who meant so much to so many was mortally ill.

I pondered his words. What had he meant by them? Was it possible to accept death so easily? Death. Faceless enemy, fearsome monster who devours our days, confounds the philosopher, silences the poet, and reduces the mighty to offering all their gold, in vain, for yet another hour! Was he telling me not to sorrow overmuch, thinking of my feelings when he was moving toward the end of all feeling? Could he have been consoling me?

Suddenly . . . I found myself recalling a Hasidic teaching he often quoted. "There are three ascending levels of how one mourns: with tears—that is the lowest; with silence—that is higher; and with song—that is the highest."

I understood then what it was I had experienced: the lesson that how a man meets death is a sign of how he has met life. Intimations of melody countered my sadness. At that moment the power of the human spirit, mortal and frail though it is, never seemed so strong.

SAMUEL H. DRESNER

We Too

When Aaron's time came to depart from this world, the Holy One said to Moses, "Go tell Aaron of his impending death." So Moses rose early in the morning and went to Aaron. As soon as he called out, "Aaron, my brother," Aaron came down and asked, "What made you come here so early today?"

Moses replied, "During the night I meditated on a matter in Scripture which I found distressing, and so I rose early and came to you."

"What was the matter?" Aaron asked.

"I do not remember, but I know it was in the Book of Genesis. Bring it and we'll read it."

They took the Book of Genesis, read each and every section in it, and said about each one of them, "The Holy One wrought well, created well." But when they came to the creation of Adam, Moses asked, "What is one to say of Adam, who brought death to the world, so that I, who prevailed over the ministering angels, and you, who held back death—are not even you and I to have a like end? After all, how many more years have we to live?"

"Not many," Aaron answered.

Moses continued talking, until finally he mentioned to him the precise day when death was to come. At that moment, Aaron's bones felt the imminence of his own demise. So he asked, "Is it because of me that you found the matter in Scripture so distressing?"

Moses answered, "Yes."

At once Israel noticed that Aaron's height had diminished, even as it says, "My heart writhes within me; and the terrors of death are fallen upon me" (Psalm 55:5).

Moses asked, "Is dying acceptable to you?"
"Yes."
"Then let us go up on the mountain."

Yalkut Shim'oni

Leavetaking

Leavetaking

For Even a Moment

Lord, all my longing is before You,
Even though it does not pass my lips.
Grant me Your favor for even a moment,
And I will die. If only You would grant my wish!
I will commit my spirit into Your keeping,
I will sleep, and my sleep will be pleasant.
When I am far from You my life is death;
But if I cling to You, my death is life.
But I do not know what to offer You,
What my service and my worship should be.

Show me Your ways, O Lord,
Restore me from the bondage of folly.
Teach me while I still have the strength to
    endure—
Do not scorn my plight!—
Before I become a burden to myself
And my limbs weigh heavy on each other;
Before I yield unwillingly, and my bones
Wither and are unable to bear me;
Before I journey to where my fathers have
    gone,
And come to rest where they are resting.

I am like a stranger upon the earth,
But my true home is in her womb.

YEHUDAH HALEVI

To the End

On the Great Sabbath, not many days before he died, Rabbi Moshe of Kobryn repeated the words of the psalm over and over again: "Praise the Lord, O my soul!" Then he added softly, "Soul of mine, you will praise the Lord in every world, no matter in what world you are. But this is what I beg of God: 'I will praise the Lord while I live'—as long as I still live here, I want to be able to praise Him."

On the last day of Passover he talked at table a long time before grace was said. Then he concluded, "Now I have nothing more to say. Let us say grace."

On the following night he lay down on his deathbed, and he died a week later.

HASIDIC LORE

111

In the Time Remaining

Rabbi David Leikes lived more than a hundred years. He was esteemed as an authority on rabbinic civil law, and his decisions were admired by all the judges.

Once, when the aged rabbi was on his deathbed, a very complicated case arose. His demise was expected any moment. The judges hoped that the ancient rabbi's mind might still be sufficiently clear to aid them, perhaps for the last time. They visited his home and stated their request. The rabbi's children protested vigorously and argued against troubling him, lest thereby his end be hastened.

Suddenly the door opened, and the dying rabbi entered. "Did you know," he said, "that we are taught by the Talmud [*Shabbat* 10] that one who judges a case correctly becomes thereby God's partner? Yet you wish to deprive me of this opportunity!"

He gave his decision in the difficult case in a manner so remarkable that it left no doubt as to its correctness. He returned to his bed with the help of his children, and a moment later he died.

HASIDIC LORE

Not to Be Idle

The soul of Rabbi Yitzhak Meir, author of *Hiddushei Harim*, departed on the Sabbath at twilight, the hour of grace.

Sitting in his chair, he rinsed his hands for the Third Meal, then broke bread, said the benediction, and took a taste. Suddenly his face began to change, and all those present saw that the hour of his departure had come. Everyone began crying, and there was a great commotion.

Rabbi Yitzhak Meir noticed that one of his grandsons, a young lad, was standing idly by. He called him over and said to him, "While they're all busy weeping, you are neglecting the study of the Torah. Bring a volume of the Talmud, and I'll give you a lesson."

After this, he covered his face with his ritual vest and departed for eternal life.

HASIDIC LORE

113

Let Me Be Quiet

In my great loneliness, the loneliness of a
   wounded animal,
I lie, hour after hour, unspeaking.
Fate has harvested my vineyard, leaving not a
   grape,
But the submissive heart is forgiving.
If these days be my last,
Let me be quiet,
That my bitterness not sully the quiet blue
Of the sky, ever my companion.

RAHEL

All Night I Wept

All night I wept
Master of the Universe
Might there not be a death without
Violence
Death like a flower.
All night I poured out my pleas
Though I be but dust
Let me be restful enough
To gaze up into the highest heavens
Again and again and again
To take leave of their beauty,

All night I thought
Many beings dwell
In my aching chest
And all kinds of stories,
I must light a candle
And look at them
Before I sleep the sleep of death.

ZELDA

115

Burn Clear

Burn out, my life, burn quick,
Not much is left now of the wick.
Let there be light on my last day,
To point the way.

Don't flicker, life, burn clear.
Then, like a spring thought, disappear.
I hate to stint! Life, blaze away!
Let me have light at least one day.

Avrohom Reisen

Whatever Is in Your Power

Go, eat your bread in gladness, and drink your wine in joy; for your action was long ago approved by God. Let your clothes always be freshly washed, and your head never lack ointment. Enjoy happiness with a woman you love all the fleeting days of life that have been granted to you under the sun—all your fleeting days. For that alone is what you can get out of life and out of the means you acquire under the sun. Whatever it is in your power to do, do with all your might. For there is no action, no reasoning, no learning, no wisdom in the netherworld, where you are going.

ECCLESIASTES

Judgment

When Rabban Yohanan ben Zakkai fell ill, his disciples went to visit him. Seeing them, he began to weep. They said to him, "Lamp of Israel, great pillar, mighty hammer, why do you weep?"

He replied: "If I were being taken today before a human king, who is here today and gone tomorrow; whose anger, if he is angry with me, does not last forever; who, if he imprisons me, does not imprison me indefinitely; who, if he puts me to death, does not put me to everlasting death; and whom I can persuade with words and bribe with money, I would still weep.

"But now that I am being taken before the supreme King of Kings, the Holy One, blessed be He, who lives and endures eternally; whose anger, if He is angry with me, is an unending anger; who, if He imprisons me, imprisons me forever; who, if He puts me to death, puts me to everlasting death; and whom I cannot persuade with words or bribe with money, . . . shall I not weep?"

BERAKHOT

Looking Back

The Rabbi of Ger once said: Why is man afraid of dying? Does he not then go to his Father? What man fears is the moment he will survey from the other world everything he has experienced on this earth.

HASIDIC LORE

The Open Hand

The gates of prayer are sometimes open and sometimes closed, but the gates of repentance are ever open. As the sea is always accessible, so is the hand of the Holy One, blessed be He, always open to receive penitents.

DEUTERONOMY RABBAH

Reckoning the Days

"And the days drew near that Israel must die" (Genesis 47:29). . . .

When God has decided to receive back a person's spirit, He passes in review all the days of the person's life in this world. And happy the one whose days draw near to pass before the King without blame, with not a single one rejected on account of any sin therein. Thus "drew near" is said of the righteous, for their days draw near to pass before the King without blame. And woe to the wicked, whose days were all spent in sin and go unrecorded above, and hence their days cannot draw near.

ZOHAR

Each Man Has a Name

Each man has a name
Given him by God
And given him by his father and mother.
Each man has a name
Given him by his stature
And his way of smiling,
And given him by his clothes.
Each man has a name
Given him by the mountains
And given him by his walls.
Each man has a name
Given him by the planets
And given him by his neighbors.
Each man has a name
Given him by his sins
And given him by his longing.
Each man has a name
Given him by his enemies
And given him by his love.
Each man has a name
Given him by his feast days
And given him by his craft.
Each man has a name

Given him by the seasons of the year
And given him by his blindness.
Each man has a name
Given him by the sea
And given him by his death.

ZELDA

One More Poem

After I am dead
Say this at my funeral:

There was a man who exists no more.

That man died before his time
And his life's song was broken off halfway.
Oh, he had one more poem
And that poem has been lost
Forever.

He had a lyre,
And a vital, quivering soul.
The poet in him spoke,
Gave out all his heart's secrets,
His hand struck all its chords.
But there was one secret he kept hidden
Though his fingers danced everywhere.
One string stayed mute
And is still soundless.
But alas! all its days
That string trembled,
Trembled softly, softly quivered

For the poem that would free her,
Yearned and thirsted, grieved and wept,
As though pining for someone expected
Who does not come,
And the more he delays, she whimpers
With a soft, fine sound,
But he does not come,
And the agony is very great,
There was a man and he exists no more.
His life's song was broken off halfway.
He had one more poem
And that poem is lost,
Forever.

HAYIM NAHMAN BIALIK

Regrets

Forgive me, O Lord,
for I have spilled my life
on the ground
like foul water.
Forgive me, for all my wounds
are self-inflicted,
and with a weeping voice
like a beaten child,
I cry out to You
that You should bind them for me,
my Lord.

MORDECAI TEMKIN

What I Could Have Been

Before his death, Rabbi Zusya of Hanipol said, "In the coming world, they will not ask me, 'Why were you not Moses?' They will ask me, 'Why were you not Zusya?'"

HASIDIC LORE

The Truth

Rabbi Elimelekh of Lizhensk once said: "I am certain to have a share in the coming world.

"When I stand in the court of justice above and they ask me, 'Have you studied all you should?' I shall answer, 'No.'

"Then they will ask, 'Have you prayed all you should?' And again I shall answer, 'No.'

"And they will put a third question to me: 'Have you done all the good you should?' And this time, too, I shall have to give the same answer.

"Then they will pronounce the verdict: 'You told the truth. For the sake of truth, you deserve a share in the coming world.'"

HASIDIC LORE

Letting Go

The Sages taught in the name of Rabbi Meir: When a man comes into the world, his fists are clenched, as though to say, "The whole world is mine, and I shall inherit it." But when he departs from the world, his hands are spread open, as if to say, "I have inherited nothing from this world."

ECCLESIASTES RABBAH

The Vineyard

"As he came out of his mother's womb, so must he depart at last, naked as he came" (Ecclesiastes 5:14).

Geniva said: The verse is to be understood by the parable of a fox who found a vineyard fenced in on all sides, except for one gap, through which he tried to enter but could not [squeeze through]. What did he do? He fasted for three days, until he became lean and slender, and thus he squeezed himself through the gap.

But after the fox had eaten [of the grapes], he became fat again, and when he wished to go out through that gap, he could not. He fasted another three days, until he once again became lean and slender. In this way, he was able to go out.

After getting out, he turned toward the vineyard and, gazing at it, said, "O vineyard, vineyard, how goodly are you, and how goodly is your fruit! All that is within you is beautiful and comely, but what benefit can one derive from you? As one goes into you, so must one come out."

Such also is the world.

ECCLESIASTES RABBAH

The Wedding Tune

Once Rabbi Moshe Leib of Sasov married off two orphans and saw to it that they did not feel deserted on their wedding day. When the two young people stood under the bridal canopy, the rabbi's face was transfigured with radiance, for at that moment he felt himself a father twice over. He listened to the tune the musicians were playing. Then he said to the people standing around him, "I wish I could be assured that I would go to my eternal home, on the day destined, to the sound of this tune."

After many years, when this hour and these words were long forgotten, a number of musicians were traveling to play at a wedding in Brody, on a snowy winter's day. Suddenly the horses began to pull harder and broke into a rapid trot. The driver could not slow them up. They went faster and faster, jolted the sleigh worse and worse, and ran unerringly toward some goal of their own. They finally stopped at a cemetery. The musicians saw many people gathered there and asked where they were and who was being buried. When they heard the name of Rabbi Moshe Leib, they remembered how, years before, when they were young, they had played before him at the wedding of the two orphans. And now the people too recalled the incident, and they all cried, "Play the wedding tune!"

HASIDIC LORE

In the House of the Lord

The Lord is my shepherd;
  I lack nothing.
He makes me lie down in green pastures;
  He leads me to water in places of repose;
  He renews my life;
  He guides me in right paths
  as befits His name.
Though I walk through the valley of the shadow of
  death,
  I fear no harm, for You are with me;
  Your rod and Your staff—they comfort me.
You spread a table for me in full view of my
  enemies;
  You anoint my head with oil;
  my drink is abundant.
Only goodness and steadfast love shall pursue me
  all the days of my life,
  and I shall dwell in the house of the Lord
  forever.

PSALMS

Final Confession

O Lord, my God and God of my fathers, You who are the creator of life and in whose hands are the spirits of all flesh, humbly and trustingly do I turn to You with my prayer. My life and my death are in Your hands. I would pray You for life and for healing in this moment of my affliction and pain. But if in Your wisdom the span of my life here is now come to an end, resignedly do I accept Your decree.

I would approach You, O heavenly Father, with clean hands and a pure heart. Yet I feel weighed down by sins against You and against my fellow men. Therefore I confess my guilt, and I trust in Your bountiful mercy, that forgives the sinner.

Fervently do I pray and sincerely do I trust that You will show me the path of life, so that, cleansed through You, my soul may enter life everlasting.

You who are the Father of the fatherless and the Protector of the helpless, watch over my loved ones. Into Your hand I commit my spirit. May You redeem it, O God of mercy and truth.

Hear O Israel: the Lord is our God, the Lord alone. The Lord, He is God. The Lord, He is God.

CCAR Manual

Appendix:
The Death of Rabbi Nahman

It was on the third day of Selihot that I arrived at Uman, planning to be there for Rosh Hashanah. I stayed there, however, until he departed from us in peace, and I merited to be present at the hour of his holy and awesome death. . . .

It had always been his way to say words of Torah at the close of the first day of Rosh Hashanah. A great crowd had gathered in the large house which had been designated for that purpose, and the room where he was to speak was already packed with people. Evening began to fall as we waited for him to appear, but he was near death and did not have the strength to enter the room. While we were standing there, a message came that he had called for me. I left the crowd and went to the place where he was staying.

I found him seated on the edge of his bed, with a brass bowl beside him; the bowl was fast filling up with blood. As soon as he saw me enter, he cried out to me, "What shall I do about my teaching?" My first reaction was that there was nothing to be done; surely he could not go to teach in that condition. But he persisted, saying how sorry he felt for the people who had gone through such great difficulties in order to hear him. [How could he refuse them?] All summer long he had been looking forward to this Rosh Hashanah, when he would say Torah in Uman. Then I understood how deeply he longed to teach. I began

137

to say to him, "When you returned from your journey to Lemberg you were also very weak, and there seemed to be no natural way that you would have the strength to teach. Yet on that occasion God was with you and you managed to speak at great length." I kept saying things of this sort for a while, until he finally responded, "I'm willing to give my life for it." . . . And it really was at the risk of his life that he would go to teach; he seemed about to die at any moment. . . .

He came into the room and sat down on his chair, and we all stood around him. The room was really so terribly filled with people that it was hard to be there at all. People were almost standing on top of one another; the crowding and noise were so awful that some people became faint and had to be taken out. . . . But he sat there in the midst of the crowd, waited a while before he spoke, as was his custom, and then began to speak. . . . His voice was so much lower than usual that it seemed impossible that he could go on for long. But the God of mercy had compassion upon us and upon all Israel and upon all the generations to come, and he was able to continue, as though by the most wondrous miracle. . . . When he finished, he had us sing a *niggun* [wordless melody], as we always did on such occasions, and he went back to his room. . . .

On the second day of Rosh Hashanah, he did not come in to pray with us or to join us in the meal, as was his custom on that holiday. He stayed in his own adjoining room and there he prayed alone. And though he was weak beyond description in those days following Rosh Hashanah, he managed to speak to each of the people who had come to be with him, giving to each of them according to his needs. As people came to take leave of him after the holiday, he spoke to each at length. It was because of this show of strength that people did not realize he was so near death; otherwise they never would have left him. Even his own daughters and his son-in-law went home after the holiday, never imagining that he was to die so soon. Had we really paid attention to what was happening, we would have realized that he lived each moment only by miracle.

He himself said to us countless times and in numerous ways that he was about to die. But we, sinful creatures that we are, could not believe that God would take this pure light from us at such a time. We lost so much by not accepting that his death was near. How much more would we have wanted to hear from him, had we only known! We can only give thanks to God, who in His mercy allowed us to hear sufficient teachings from our master to nourish all the future generations . . . until the end of time. . . .

On the eve of Yom Kippur, we went in to him, and he blessed each one of us, as was his custom. His appearance, however, was somehow frightening, so that an awesome sense of shame overtook us all. How hard it is to describe his face as it was at that moment of receiving his blessing, for he had a holy and awesome glow about him. Truly blessed are we, who were able to receive that final blessing from him before he died. . . .

When we returned to his room after the fast was over, we found him very weak and of sad demeanor. The next morning, however, his mood was improved, and he spoke joyfully with people. . . . It was on that day that he had to change his dwelling, returning to the house where he had lived before Rosh Hashanah. . . . As we began to move his possessions into the new apartment and to arrange things in their proper order, he became especially concerned about where we should place his bed. Wherever we tried somehow did not seem right to him. Finally, I tried moving a chest of drawers and placed the bed where the chest had stood. This seemed right to him. . . . Only afterwards, when he died on that bed in that place, did I understand that the precise place where he was to die had been designated years before, and was somehow known to him. . . .

On that Monday evening, the eve of the last day of his life, his disciples Reb Naftali and Reb Shim'on stood before him (for we were sleeping in shifts, so that he was never left alone). . . . The two disciples were overcome by a combination of terror and sadness, realizing that he was so directly preparing for his death. One of them whispered something about it to the other, but the master overheard. "Why are you whispering?" he said. "You can speak of my death to my face. I'm not afraid of it.". . .

When I awoke . . . Naftali whispered to me a bit of what had happened—that he had already given them the key and told them to burn his writings. I stood there, shaking with disbelief. But then I pulled myself together, convincing myself that this was just his way. He might be preparing for death, but surely God wouldn't take him. We could not get it into our minds that God would take this great light . . . before all those who needed him had gotten a chance to enjoy his wondrous and awesome light.

We poor sinners lost so much because of thoughts like these! If only we could have simply believed that he was going to die, as he said to us so many times, both directly and indirectly, we could have heard so much more from him in that hour. He was waiting for us to ask him that he tell us more. But we were not willing to hear anything that might concern what we were to do after his death; our only hope was that he get well again. And since we didn't ask, he told us nothing more. . . .

I stood there before him, I alone, from shortly after midnight until we saw the light of dawn. But I heard nothing from him in all those hours—all because I did not want to accept that he was dying, and I asked him nothing. . . . He looked into me with his awesome eyes, and every look contained countless words. Now I understand so much about the looks he gave me that night, and whenever I pass through times of suffering, and God saves me through His wonders, I understand that it was all there in his eyes, in the intensity with which he stared at me, for hours at a time, during that final night. . . .

When dawn broke and the others were awakened . . . I left to go to the *mikvah* [ritual bath] before my prayers on that fourth day of Sukkot. Upon my return I found him sitting up on the bed, wrapped in his *tallit* [prayer shawl] and saying his prayers. He then took the *lulav* and *etrog* [frond and citron] in his hands and with the prayerbook of the Ari, may his memory be a blessing, resting on his knees, he recited the Hallel. When he came to the Hosha'not he raised his voice a bit, so that his prayers could be heard throughout the house. Happy are the eyes that saw him, happy are the ears that heard his prayers, on that last day of his holy life. . . .

[A short while later], he was seated on his chair, but life was quickly passing out of him. People were standing over him with various kinds of fragrant spices, to restore his soul. God had also caused a certain man from Tirhavits to be there on that day, and he was attending to him above all the others.

142

(Here, too, there is a tale to tell, for our master had already promised this man that he would be present on the day of his death.) When I saw the scene, I told them to put him to bed immediately, but our master himself waved me aside. Only a bit later, when I saw that sitting up was totally impossible for him, did I repeat my words. This time he was silent and did not resist. The man from Tirhavits took him in his arms and laid him on the bed. As he put him down, I took his holy hand in mine, first as in a greeting, but then in embrace, as a sign of the bond between us.

He lay on his bed, dressed in a fine silken garment, which he had asked Reb Shim'on to put around him. He asked that his sleeves be buttoned, and when a bit of his shirtsleeve still showed out from under his coat, he motioned that it be set right. He then asked that we wash off his beard, for there was a bit of blood stuck to it. He lay there in great freedom. . . .

It took about three hours from the time he was laid down on the bed. . . . The house was filled with people who had come to honor him. When they saw that the end was near, they began to recite the *Ma'avar Yabok* [Crossing the Jabbok], the [book of] verses one recites at the death of a *tzaddik*. It then seemed that he was already dead, and the people began to weep. I cried out, "Master! Master! To whom do you leave us?" He heard our voice and awoke, turning his face to us as though to say, "God forbid! I'm not leaving you!" But just a bit after that, he died and was gathered unto his people, in holiness and purity, with no confusion of mind and without the slightest gesture, with an acceptance that was awesome and wondrous. All those who stood about him, the leaders of the burial society among them, said that they had seen many who had passed on in pure and conscious ways but they had never seen a death like this.

Now all this is told only according to our understanding. As to the true meaning of his death—there are no words to describe it, for it surpasses all understanding. Only those who know a bit of his greatness, who have read his holy books or have heard his stories, will begin to realize that his death was completely unique. There was never any like it, nor will there ever be. How shall we speak? What shall we say? What shall I say to the Lord, who gave me the gift of being there as his holy soul passed out of him? Had I only come into the world for the sake of this moment, it would have been sufficient.

RABBI NATHAN OF NEMIROV

Sources by Page Number

Abbreviations

BL = Hayim Nahman Bialik and Yehoshua Hana Ravnit-zky, *The Book of Legends: Sefer Ha-aggadah*, trans. William G. Braude (New York: Schocken, 1992).

C = T. Carmi, ed. and trans., *The Penguin Book of Hebrew Verse* (New York: Penguin and Viking, 1981).

G = *The Psalms: A New Translation*, trans. Joseph Geli-neau (London: The Grail, 1963).

H = Binyamin Mintz, *Sefer Hahistalkut* (The Book of Departing) (Tel Aviv: Ketubim, 1930).

MS = Michael Swirsky.

R = Rahel (Bluwstein), *Shirat Rahel* (The Poetry of Rahel) (Tel Aviv: Davar, 1981).

T = *Tanakh: The Holy Scriptures* (Philadelphia: Jewish Publication Society, 1962–1982).

TH = Martin Buber, ed., *Tales of the Hasidim* (New York: Schocken, 1948).

Z = Zelda (Mishkovsky), *Shirei Zelda* (Zelda's Poems) (Tel Aviv: Hakibbutz Hameuchad, 1985).

Note: Texts for which no publisher is given were trans-lated by Michael Swirsky. Unless otherwise identified, all references to talmudic tractates are in the Baby-lonian Talmud.

P. 3, **A Time for Everything**—Ecclesiastes 3:1–8 (T).

P. 4, **Over Like a Sigh**—Psalm 90:1–12 (G).

P. 6, **The Spoiler**— *"Keter malkhut"* (The Royal Crown), stanza 37. Trans. MS.

P. 9, **At the Abyss**—*"Al sfat tehom shel kiyumkha"* (At the Edge of the Abyss of Your Existence), in Pinhas Sadeh, *Ikh zing vi a feigele: shirim 1989–1992* (I Sing Like a Bird: Poems, 1989–1992) (Jerusalem and Tel Aviv: Schocken, 1993), 35. Trans. MS.

P. 10, **Life and Death Are Brothers**—*Duties of the Heart*, from the appendix "Reproof," in *Returning: Exercises in Repentance*, ed. and trans. Jonathan Magonet (London: Reform Synagogues of Great Britain, 1975), 79.

P. 12, **A Narrow Bridge**—*Meshivat nafesh* (Restoring the Soul). (New York: Eliezer Shlomo Breslaver, 1965), 14. Trans. MS.

P. 13, **Living toward Death**—"Das Buchlein vom gesunden und kranken Menschenverstand" (A Treatise on Healthy and Unhealthy Thinking), trans. Francis C. Golffing, in *Franz Rosenzweig: His Life and Thought*, ed. Nahum N. Glatzer (New York: Schocken, 1953), 211–213.

P. 15, **Beyond Time**—*Meshivat nafesh*, op. cit., 84. Trans. MS.

P. 16, **Surviving as a Thought of God**—"Reflections on Death," *Conservative Judaism* 28:1 (Fall 1973), p. 3.

P. 19, **The Living**—*Tanhuma* (Buber ed.), Berakhah 28b ff., in *A Rabbinic Anthology*, ed. and trans. C. G. Montefiore and H. Loewe (Philadelphia: Jewish Publication Society, 1960), 580–581.

P. 20, **With Our Lives We Give Life**—*Gates of Prayer* (New York: Central Conference of American Rabbis, 1975), 626–627.

P. 21, **Parents and Children**—*Baba Batra* 116a.

P. 22, **The People's Soul**—*The Religion of Reason out of the Sources of Judaism*, trans. Simon Kaplan (New York: Ungar, 1972), 301.

P. 23, **The Chain of the Generations**—*Ta'anit* 23a.

P. 24, **Repaying God**—Heschel, "Reflections on Death."

P. 27, **Against Your Will**—selected from *Tanhuma*, Pekudei 3, trans. in BL, 575–576, sec. 7.

P. 30, **Departing**—*Zohar*, Vayehi 223b; 2 *Barukh* 14:5.

P. 31, **Pleading for Time**—selected from *Deuteronomy Rabbah* 7:10, 11:10; *Tanhuma*, Va'ethanan 6; *Yalkut Shim'oni*, Va'ethanan 821, trans. in BL, 101–104.

P. 37, **What Is the Measure of My Days?**—Psalm 39: 3–8 (T).

P. 38, **The Angel of Death at Bay**—*Shabbat* 30a–b; *Ecclesiastes Rabbah* 5:10, para. 2, trans. in BL, 122.

P. 40, **The Fears of the Righteous**—adapted from TH, vol. 2, 171.

P. 41, **Alive He Shall Acknowledge You**—*"Hai hai hu yodekha,"* in Z, 135. Trans. MS.

P. 42, **From the Grave, Who Can Give You Praise?**—Psalm 6:3–8 (G).

P. 43, **What Is to Be Gained from My Death?**— Psalm 30:7–11 (T).

P. 44, **Is It for Your Sake?**—TH, vol. 1, 212–213.

P. 46, **Consider My Sorrows with My Sins**—*"Keter malkhut"* (The Royal Crown), stanza 38. Trans. MS.

P. 49, **God Is Against Me**: Lamentations 3:1–9 (T).

P. 50, **Better to Die**—Job 3:3–4, 20–26, 6:8–11 (T).

P. 52, **Look Away from Me!**—Job 7:17–21 (T).

P. 53, **I Cry to You in Vain**—Job 30:15–23 (T).

P. 57, **Heal Me and I Shall Be Healed**—"Atah hu hashem" (You Are the Lord), in Yig'al Shafran, *Leket tefillot haholeh* (A Collection of Prayers for the Sick) (Jerusalem: Jerusalem Religious Council, 1992), 13–18. Trans. MS.

P. 59, **All My Body Is Sick**—Psalm 38:2–11, 22–23 (G).

P. 61, **To Feel the Darkness**—trans. Maurice Samuel, in *The Plough Woman*, ed. Rahel Katznelson-Rubashow (New York: Nicholas L. Brown, 1932), 280.

P. 62, **Through the Openings**—*"Nafshi hetzitzah min haharakim,"* in Z, 229. Trans. MS.

P. 63, **I Am Sinking**—Psalm 69:2–4, 15–18 (G).

P. 65, **Restore Me to Health**—adapted from an anonymous prayer in *Help and Comfort*, ed. Morris A. Gutstein et al. (Chicago: Chicago Board of Rabbis, 1960).

P. 67, **Withered like the Grass**—Psalm 102:2–12 (G).

P. 69, **Until Your Purpose Is Fulfilled**—adapted from an anonymous work composed at a women's prayer workshop, in *When the Body Hurts, the Soul Still Longs to Sing* (San Francisco: Jewish Healing Center, 1992).

P. 71, **Comfort Me**—trans. Maurice Samuel, in Katznelson-Rubashow, op. cit., 279.

P. 72, **The Help of Others**—*Song of Songs Rabbah* 2:16, trans. in Montefiore and Loewe, 549–550, para. 1542.

P. 74, **Be Good to Me**—*"Heyeh na tov elai,"* in R, 56. Trans. MS.

P. 75, **My Soul Is Bitter**—from *Likkutei tefillot* (Selected Prayers of Rabbi Nahman of Bratslav). Trans. MS.

P. 77, **Let Him Go**—*Ketubot* 104a.

P. 78, **Beloved of My Soul**—"*Yedid nefesh*," C, 471–472.

P. 83, **Do Not Despair!**—from descriptions by his followers of an appearance by Rabbi Nahman not long before his death, in *Sihot haran* 153, trans. Arthur Green, in his *Tormented Master: A Life of Rabbi Nahman of Bratslav* (New York: Schocken, 1981), 263–265.

P. 85, **For Good and Bad Alike**—Mishnah *Berakhot* 9:5; *Berakhot* 60b, trans. in BL, 715, para. 300; Pinhas Sadeh, ed., *Ish beheder sagur, libo shavur, uvahutz yoredet afelah* (A Man in a Closed Room, His Heart Broken, and Darkness Falling Outside) (Tel Aviv: Schocken, 1993), 48. Trans. MS.

P. 87, **Can Suffering Be Good?**—*Genesis Rabbah* 9:8, trans. in BL, 716, para. 303; *Sanhedrin* 101a–b; see also *Sifrei Deuteronomy* 32 and *Yalkut* on 2 Kings 226, trans. in BL, 716, para. 306.

P. 89, **Closer to God**—*Ta'anit* 8a; *Berakhot* 5a; *Tanhuma*, Ki Tetze 2; *Kiddushin* 40b.

P. 90, **Pain Scrubs the Soul**—TH, vol. 2, 102; *Berakhot* 5a.

P. 91, **Into the Palace**—*Zohar* 1:244b, trans. in *Zohar: The Book of Splendor*, ed. and trans. Gershom G. Scholem (New York: Schocken, 1949), 72–73.

P. 93, **The Height of Knowledge**—*Guide of the Perplexed* 3:51, trans. Nahum N. Glatzer in *A Jewish Reader*, ed. Nahum N. Glatzer (New York: Schocken, 1946), 63–64.

P. 94, **To See God**—H, 17; TH, vol. 2, 148.

P. 96, **The Next Room**—TH, vol. 2, 302; Palestinian Talmud, *Yevamot* 57a.

P. 97, **Into the Harbor**—*Exodus Rabbah* 48:1 and *Ecclesiastes Rabbah* 7:1, trans. in BL, 583, para. 78.

P. 99, **At the Proper Time**—*Song of Songs Rabbah* 6, in *The Talmudic Anthology*, ed and trans. Louis I. Newman (New York: Behrman House, 1945), 90.

P. 100, **Why Should I Not Rejoice?**—TH, vol. 2, 268; H, 39; *The Hasidic Anthology*, ed. Louis I. Newman (New York and London: Scribner's, 1938), 70.

P. 102, **Willingly**—TH, vol. 1, 156–157.

P. 103, **Take Me, O Lord**—*I Asked for Wonder: A Spiritual Anthology*, ed. Samuel Dresner (New York: Crossroad, 1987), vii–viii.

P. 105, **We Too**—*Yalkut Shim'oni*, Hukkat 464, trans. in BL, 94, para. 107.

P. 109, **For Even a Moment**—prayer for Yom Kippur, trans. in C, 336.

P. 111, **To the End**—TH, vol. 2, 173.

P. 112, **In the Time Remaining**—originally in *Fun rebns hof*, ed. D. L. Mekler; *The Hasidic Anthology*, op. cit., 72, trans. Louis I. Newman (New York, 1931).

P. 113, **Not to Be Idle**—H, 35.

P. 114, **Let Me Be Quiet**—R, 25.

P. 115, **All Night I Wept**—"*Kol halaylah bakhiti*," in Z, 122. Trans. MS.

P. 116, **Burn Clear**—trans. Joseph Leftwich, in *The Golden Peacock*, ed. Joseph Leftwich (Cambridge, MA: Sci-Art, 1939).

P. 117, **Whatever Is in Your Power**—Ecclesiastes 9: 7–10 (T).

P. 118, **Judgment**—*Berakhot* 28b.

P. 119, **Looking Back**—TH, vol. 2, 311.

P. 120, **The Open Hand**—*Deuteronomy Rabbah*, trans. in Magonet, op. cit., 32.

P. 121, **Reckoning the Days**—*Zohar* I: 221b, trans. in Scholem, op. cit., 60.

P. 122, **Each Man Has a Name**—trans. in C, 558.

P. 124, **One More Poem**—"After My Death," trans. A. C. Jacobs, in *Anthology of Modern Hebrew Poetry*, ed. S. Y. Penueli and A. Ukhmani (Jerusalem: Israel Universities Press, 1966).

P. 126, **Regrets**—"Foul Water," translated from the Yiddish by Jeremy Garber in *Voices Within the Ark*, ed. Howard Schwartz and Anthony Rudolph (New York: Avon, 1980), 19.

P. 127, **What I Could Have Been**—TH, vol. 1, 251.

P. 128, **The Truth**—TH, vol. 1, 253.

P. 129, **Letting Go**—*Ecclesiastes Rabbah* 5:14, para. 1, trans. in BL, 583, para. 75.

P. 130, **The Vineyard**—*Ecclesiastes Rabbah* 5:14, trans. in BL, 583, para. 76.

P. 131, **The Wedding Tune**—TH, vol. 2, 93–94.

P. 133, **In the House of the Lord**—Psalm 23 (T, adapted).

P. 134, **Final Confession**—*CCAR Manual* (New York: Central Conference of American Rabbis, 1961), 59.

P. 135, **The Death of Rabbi Nahman**—*Yemei maharnat*, 71ff., trans. Arthur Green, in *Conservative Judaism* 28:1 (Fall 1973), p. 81 ff.

Descriptive Index of Sources

Numbers in parentheses indicate pages in the present book where the following sources are cited.

Exodus Rabbah (97): 8th- to 10th-century midrash on Exodus.

Gates of Prayer (20): 20th-century American Reform prayer book.

Genesis Rabbah (87): 5th-century midrash on Genesis.

Help and Comfort (65): 20th-century American book of prayers for the sick.

Heschel, Abraham Joshua (16, 24): 20th-century theologian and scholar (Poland, Germany, and United States).

Ibn Gabirol, Solomon (6, 46): 11th-century Hebrew poet and philosopher (Spain).

Job (50, 52, 53): book of the Hebrew Bible.

Ketubot (77): tractate of the Talmud.

Kiddushin (89): tractate of the Talmud.

Lamentations (49): book of the Hebrew Bible.

Maimonides (93): Rabbi Moshe ben Maimon (Rambam), 12th-century rabbinical scholar, philosopher, and physician (Spain, Morocco, and Egypt).

Menahem Mendel of Kotsk, Rabbi (86): 19th-century Hasidic sage (Poland).

Mishnah (85): 2nd-century code of law, core of the Talmud.

Nahman of Bratslav, Rabbi (12, 15, 75): 18th- to 19th-century Hasidic sage (Ukraine).

Nathan of Nemirov, Rabbi (84, 137): leading disciple of Rabbi Nahman of Bratslav (q.v.).

Palestinian Talmud (96): 3rd- to 4th-century compilation of rabbinical legal discourse and lore.

Psalms (4, 37, 42, 43, 59, 63, 67, 133): book of the Hebrew Bible.

Rahel (61, 71, 74, 114): pen name of Rahel Bluwstein, 20th-century Hebrew poet and pioneer (Russia and Palestine).

Reisen, Avrohom (116): 19th- to 20th-century Yiddish poet and short-story writer (Russia, Poland, and United States).

Rosenzweig, Franz (13): 20th-century philosopher (Germany).

Saadya Gaon (57): 10th-century philosopher and rabbinical scholar (Babylonia).

Sadeh, Pinhas (9): 20th-century Hebrew poet, novelist, and anthologist (Israel).

Sanhedrin (87): tractate of the Talmud.

Shabbat (38): tractate of the Talmud.

Sihot Haran (83): collection of teachings of Rabbi Nahman of Bratslav (q.v.).

Song of Songs Rabbah (72, 99): 11th-century midrash on the Song of Songs.

Ta'anit (23, 89): tractate of the Talmud.

Tanhuma (19, 27, 31, 89): 8th- to 9th-century midrash on the Pentateuch.

Temkin, Mordecai (126): 20th-century Hebrew poet (Poland and Palestine/Israel).

When the Body Hurts, the Soul Still Longs to Sing (69): 20th-century American book of prayers for the sick.

Yalkut Shim'oni (31, 105): 13th-century midrashic anthology.

Yehudah Halevi (109): 11th- to 12th-century poet and philosopher (Spain).

Yevamot (96): tractate of the Talmud.

Zelda (41, 62, 115, 122): pen name of Zelda Mishkovsky, 20th-century Hebrew poet (Palestine/Israel).

Zohar (30, 91, 121): 13th-century collection of mystical midrashim and other teachings, central work of the Kabbalah.

For Further Reading

Abrahams, Israel. *Hebrew Ethical Wills*. Philadelphia: Jewish Publication Society, 1926.

Baeck, Leo. *The Essence of Judaism*. New York: Schocken, 1948, pp. 184–190.

Bregman, Philip. *A Handbook for Rabbis Counseling Terminal Patients*. Master's thesis, Hebrew Union College–Jewish Institute of Religion, 1975.

Broyard, Anatole. "Good Books About Being Sick," *New York Times Book Review*, April 1, 1990, pp. 28–29.

Cohen, Arthur A. "Resurrection of the Dead." In *Contemporary Jewish Religious Thought*, ed. Arthur A. Cohen and Paul Mendes-Flohr, pp. 807–813. New York: Scribner's, 1987.

Falk, Ze'ev. "The Death of the Righteous." In *The Dying Human*, ed. Amnon Carmi and Andre DeVries, pp. 287–292. Ramat-Gan: Turtledove, 1979.

Frankl, Viktor. "Facing the Transitoriness of Human Existence." *Generations* (Fall 1990).

Gates of Healing. New York: Central Conference of American Rabbis, 1988.

Greenberg, Simon. *A Jewish Philosophy and Pattern of Life* (chap. 22). New York: Jewish Theological Seminary of America, 1981.

Harlow, Jules. *The Bond of Life: A Book for Mourners*. New York: Rabbinical Assembly, 1975.

Klein, Isaac. *A Time to Be Born, A Time to Die*. New York: United Synagogue of America, 1976.

Krauss, Pesach, and Goldfischer, Morrie. *Why Me?: Coping With Grief, Loss, and Change*. New York: Bantam, 1988.

Kushner, Harold. *When Bad Things Happen to Good People*. New York: Schocken, 1981.

Lamm, Maurice. *The Jewish Way in Death and Mourning*. New York: Jonathan David, 1969.

Laytner, Anson. *Arguing with God*. Northvale, NJ: Jason Aronson, 1990, pp. 63–66.

Olan, Levi A. *Judaism and Immortality*. New York: Union of American Hebrew Congregations, 1971.

Porrath, Samuel. *Life Beyond the Final Curtain: Death Is Not the End*. Hoboken, NJ: Ktav, 1985.

Raphael, Simcha Paull. *Jewish Views of the Afterlife*. Northvale, N J: Jason Aronson, 1994.

Riemer, Jack, ed. *Jewish Reflections on Death*. New York: Schocken, 1974.

Riemer, Jack, and Stampfer, Nathaniel. *So That Your Values Live On: Ethical Wills and How to Prepare Them*. Woodstock, VT: Jewish Lights, 1991.

Rosner, Fred, ed. and trans. *Moses Maimonides' Treatise on Resurrection*. New York: Ktav, 1982.

Schachter-Shalomi, Zalman. "Life in the Hereafter: A Tour of What's to Come." In *The Jewish Almanac*, ed. Richard Siegel and Carl Rheins, pp. 594–596. New York: Bantam, 1979.

Schur, Tsvi S. *Illness and Crisis: Coping the Jewish Way*. New York: National Conference of Synagogue Youth, 1987.

Silverman, Morris, ed. *Prayers of Consolation*. Bridgeport, CT: Prayer Book Press, 1972.

Singer, Aaron M. "Human Responses to Suffering in Rabbinic Teaching." *Dialogue and Alliance* 3:3 (Fall 1989): 49–63.

Soloveitchik, Aaron. "A Glimpse of Eternity from a Hospital Dungeon." *Tradition* 21:3 (Fall 1984): 1.

Sonsino, Rifat, and Syme, Daniel B. *What Happens After I Die?: Jewish Views of Life After Death*. Northvale, NJ: Jason Aronson, 1994.

Vidaver, H. *The Book of Life*. Cincinnati and Chicago: Bloch, 1878.

Weiss, Abner. *Death and Bereavement: A Halakhic Guide*. New York: Union of Orthodox Jewish Congregations of America, 1991.

When the Body Hurts, the Soul Still Longs to Sing. San Francisco: Jewish Healing Center, n.d.

Wittenberg, Jonathan, et al., *With Healing on Its Wings: Contemplations in Times of Illness*. London: Masorti Publications, n.d.

Acknowledgments

The author gratefully acknowledges permission from the following sources to reprint previously published material. Every effort has been made to ascertain the owners of copyrights for selections in this volume and to obtain permission to reprint copyrighted passages. The author will be pleased, in any subsequent editions, to correct any inadvertent error or omission that may be pointed out.

Three poems from THE PENGUIN BOOK OF HEBREW VERSE, edited and translated by T. Carmi (Allen Lane, 1981) copyright © T. Carmi, 1981: "For The Day of Atonement" by Judah Halevi, "Beloved of My Soul" by Eliezer Azikri, and "Each Man Has A Name" by Zelda. Reproduced by permission of Penguin Books Ltd., London.

From *The Psalms: A New Translation* by Joseph Gelineau, copyright © Collins Fontana 1963. Used by permission of Collins Fontana, an imprint of HarperCollins Publishers Limited.

"When the Fig Is Ripe," from *The Talmudic Anthology* (1945), edited and translated by Louis I. Newman. Used by permission of Behrman House.

From *Tormented Master: A Life of Rabbi Nahman of Bratslav,* by Arthur Green, copyright © 1979 Univer-

162

About the Editor

Michael Swirsky is a rabbi, educator, and writer with a lifelong interest in adult Jewish spiritual growth. After graduating from the Jewish Theological Seminary of America, he was active in the beginnings of the *havurah* movement in the United States and went on to found the Pardes Institute of Jewish Studies in Jerusalem. He has taught at Brandeis University and the Hebrew University, where he developed the widely used Melton adult-Jewish-studies curriculum. Among his published works are several anthologies of Jewish religious texts and translations of S. Y. Agnon (*Present at Sinai*), Adin Steinsaltz (*Teshuvah, Woman of Valor*), and a number of other leading Hebrew authors. A resident of Jerusalem, he is currently writing on the historical roots of contemporary Israeli culture.